ENDORSEMENTS

Dreams and visions are the supernatural language of the last days. So what can we expect in the days ahead? God Himself gave us the best prophetic outlook for what's on the horizon: "In the last days, says God, I will pour out My Spirit on all flesh." Joel 2, confirmed by the apostle Peter in Acts 2, clearly shows that God's target is for *all flesh* to experience the outpouring of the Holy Spirit. Gina Gholston's book *Dreams of Awakening* is a prophetic alarm clock that reminds us what time it is in the Spirit and actually shows us how to step into this catalytic moment in history!

—Larry Sparks
Publisher, Destiny Image
Author, *Accessing the Greater Glory*

We are living in the most exciting time in church history. For those who have ears to hear, the Spirit of God is releasing a wakeup call, a prophetic call to this generation. Gina Gholston's significant new book, *Dreams of Awakening*, is a timely collection of prophetic messages that will encourage the Church to be reawakened and set ablaze with revival fire. I believe we are on the verge of the greatest move of God that the world has ever seen!

—Dr. Ché Ahn
President, Harvest International Ministry
Senior Pastor, Harvest Rock Church, Pasadena, CA
International Chancellor, Wagner University
Founder, Ché Ahn Media

We are at the beginning of the greatest awakening in the history of Christianity. The waves of revival are cresting, and many are responding with a tangible *yes*. Holy Spirit is increasing in palpable moves of fire and glory. We learn in Scripture that fire falls on sacrifice. In this time of revival and awakening, our *yes* to Him—our yielding and surrendering to Him—becomes the sacrifice on which His fire falls. Instead of looking at the burning bush, we become the burning bush—burning ones for Him. Gina has captured this message and heart of revival and awakening. The dreams given to her by the Lord, shared within *Dreams of Awakening*, will challenge and fill you with faith to cry out, "Here am I, Lord! Bend me, Lord!" You will be empowered into a life ignited on fire for Holy Spirit and given the Kingdom tools, faith, and strategy necessary to stand for awakening within our nation and the nations. Thank you, Gina, for sharing this now word filled with prophetic revelation, Holy Spirit empowerment, and Kingdom blueprints for the new era.

—Rebecca Greenwood
Co-founder, Christian Harvest International
Strategic Prayer Apostolic Network
International Freedom Group

Wow! I've never been more encouraged about where we are as Christ's Ekklesia in the earth as I am at this moment after having read Gina Gholston's new book, *Dreams of Awakening!* This book is a must in every believer's war chest. Gina takes us out of the dismay and chaos of trying to have a perspective from earth into Heaven. By sharing her prophetic dreams, interpretations, and words she gives us Heaven's perspective of what Holy Spirit is doing and about to do on earth! Do yourself a great service and read this book immediately!

—Dr. Dwain Miller
Senior Pastor, Cross Life Church of Little Rock

Our friend Gina Gholston is a gift to the Ekklesia. Her keen prophetic insight coupled with the dreams God gives her bring fresh oil to the new era we have entered. We will ride with Him for awakening, reformation, revival where a convergence of prayers, decrees, and intercession has intersected with their moment. This book will ignite and inspire you. Let the wind blow, let the fire fall, let the rain come down! It is time.

—Tim Sheets, Apostle
Author of *Angel Armies*, *Planting the Heavens*, *New Era of Glory*, and more

We are entering into one of the greatest awakenings America has ever experienced. I believe that God is pouring out Kingdom strategies through dreams, visions, and revelations! Gina Gholston is not only one of the most anointed prophetic dreamers in this generation, but I believe wholeheartedly that her new book, *Dreams of Awakening,* is an invitation for every believer to engage and partner with God's plan for revival. Summer 2021, through a series of God-orchestrated events, we had the opportunity to lead revival and expand God's Kingdom in Kentucky and gather at the Red River Meeting House that Gina had seen in a dream. I think that we, as the Church, need to be on our front foot, ready to respond to the words from the prophets, and in doing so we will see an even greater victory in our efforts! I thank the Lord for bold women of faith like Gina Gholston and believe that every person who reads this book will find a prophetic clue to their role in this great awakening!

—Jessi Green
Revivalist and author of *Wildfires*
Director of Saturate Global
www.jessigreen.com

DREAMS OF AWAKENING

DREAMS OF AWAKENING

Prayers & Prophetic Dreams Announcing the Coming Move of God

GINA GHOLSTON

DESTINY IMAGE® PUBLISHERS, INC.
P.O. Box 310, Shippensburg, PA 17257-0310
"Promoting Inspired Lives."

This book and all other Destiny Image and Destiny Image Fiction books are available at Christian bookstores and distributors worldwide.

For more information on foreign distributors, call 717-532-3040.

Reach us on the Internet: www.destinyimage.com.

ISBN 13 TP: 978-0-7684-6253-1

ISBN 13 eBook: 978-0-7684-6254-8

ISBN 13 HC: 978-0-7684-6256-2

ISBN 13 LP: 978-0-7684-6255-5

For Worldwide Distribution, Printed in the U.S.A.

1 2 3 4 5 6 7 8 / 25 24 23 22 21

DEDICATION

To my momma. When I was born, you dedicated me to the Lord, and all of my life you have believed in me and encouraged me to be and to do all that God has called me to be and to do. You saw in me the things that I couldn't see in myself, and throughout the years you have lovingly, wisely, and prayerfully helped me to navigate and stay on the path of God's destiny and purposes for my life. God knew I needed you, and I'm so thankful that it was in His great plan for me to be your daughter! It is with great love and honor that I dedicate this book to you!

ACKNOWLEDGEMENTS

To Larry Sparks and everyone at Destiny Image, thank you for your kindness, prayers, encouragement, and help throughout the process of writing this book. Thank you for how you value and rightly prioritize the glory of God and His purposes.

To all of my friends and family, thank you for your love, prayers, support, and constant encouragement. I am so thankful to God for putting each one of you in my life! I love you dearly!

To Dutch and Ceci Sheets, thank you for your friendship, kindness, and wisdom. Thank you for encouraging and enabling me to share my dreams with others! And also, thank you for taking your place in the plan of God and for being such great role models for all of us to look up to and follow. Love and blessings to you both!

To those who endorsed this book, I treasure and am honored to have your friendship and support!

Most of all, I thank God for loving me and for trusting me with these dreams, visions, and prophetic words. To You, O, God, be all of the glory!

CONTENTS

FOREWORD

There are prophetic dreamers, and there are *prophetic dreamers*—JVs and varsity, amateur and professional. Gina Gholston is the latter. I jokingly told her once, "You don't dream dreams, Gina. You dream books." This is an obvious exaggeration. However, the amount of detail in Gina's dreams, along with her ability to recall it, is amazing—sometimes staggering. She is a true prophet with a very high-level gift of dreaming.

My first exposure to Gina's dreams was in 2018. Shortly before the Turnaround Conference at the Trump hotel in DC, someone gave me her "America Shall Be Saved" dream. The impact it had on me and all the conference attendees was profound. No one doubted its accuracy. We were blessed to meet Gina shortly after this, and she has since sent us many dreams. Though known for her dreams and gift of prophecy, she is also a very gifted teacher/preacher. Now, it seems, God is demonstrating that she is also a gifted writer.

Gina not only releases prophetic revelation at a high level, but she is also one who models what every spiritual leader should demonstrate, including, of course, for prophets:

- They must never stop growing in their gift and in their personal relationship with God.
- They must be knowledgeable of the scriptures.

- They should intercede and pray over their words, dreams, visions, etc., "carrying" them in intercession.
- They should be rightly aligned with apostolic ministry and work closely with them.
- They must walk in genuine humility and integrity.
- They must demonstrate a servant's heart, never pride or an entitlement mentality.

I believe the fact that Gina checks off all these boxes is one of the reasons God can trust her with such high-level dreams. The revelation and insights in *Dreams of Awakening* will do for the body of Christ what the prophetic ministries of Zechariah and Haggai did for those who rebuilt the temple in Jerusalem:

> *Then the prophets, Haggai the prophet, and Zechariah the son of Iddo, prophesied unto the Jews that were in Judah and Jerusalem in the name of the God of Israel, even unto them. Then rose up Zerubbabel the son of Shealtiel, and Jeshua the son of Jozadak, and began to build the house of God which is at Jerusalem: and with them were the prophets of God* ***helping*** *them* (Ezra 5:1-2 KJV).
>
> *And the elders of the Jews were* ***successful*** *in building through the prophecy of Haggai the prophet and Zechariah the son of Iddo. And they finished building following the command of the God of Israel and the decree of Cyrus, Darius, and Artaxerxes king of Persia* (Ezra 6:14 NASB).

Apostles and other builders cannot build as effectively without prophets "helping" them. The leaders rebuilding the Temple in Jerusalem "succeeded," in part, through the prophesying of Haggai and

Zechariah. The diversity of gifting Holy Spirit apportions to us is essential if we are to accomplish all He intends.

First Chronicles 12 tells us the tribe of Issachar "helped David in war" (verse 1). They discerned timing and strategy (verse 32). We must know *when* as well as *what,* not only in building but also in war. Any good leader knows this. David was a great leader and warrior. He would not have had the success he had, however, without the help of prophetic leaders.

Proverbs 29:18 actually says that without prophetic revelation (*chazown*) we perish (*para*). *Chazown* includes prophecy, dreams, visions—any form of prophetic revelation. *Para* means to withdraw (from work or other activities); become naked, exposed, or uncovered; be unbridled, unrestrained, or out of control; reject, avoid, or ignore counsel; be unprepared for opportunity; and more. All of these can be the side effects from a lack of prophetic revelation. Simply stated, we cannot fully succeed—indeed, we can experience disaster—without prophetic insight and revelation.

And finally, the word of the Lord creates. Often translated "make" or "produce," the Hebrew word *asah* is often used to describe the physical creation performed by God's words (see Gen. 1:7,16,25,31 and many more). It is also used to describe the power and creative ability of prophecy. In Numbers 23:19, Isaiah 55:11, and Jeremiah 1:12, *asah* describes God performing, accomplishing, and creating through words spoken by prophets. He said of His words in Isaiah 55:11, in this context spoken by the prophet Isaiah, "So also will be the word that I speak; it does not return to me unfulfilled. My word performs My purpose and fulfills the mission I sent it out to accomplish" (TPT). God's words have assignments on them and, when believed, acted on, and declared, will accomplish those assignments. They are seeds that reproduce at the timing of the Lord (see Matt. 13:3-9, 18-23).

I am grateful for the prophetic! I'm also thankful for the tremendous maturation I am witnessing among the prophets. I thank God for vessels like Gina who have submitted to the Potter's hands, allowing Him to shape and equip them for these strategic times. Prophets are maturing believers for ministry; they will also help apostles build and govern, evangelists reap the harvest, pastors shepherd and nurture, and teachers teach.

Glean all you can from this seasoned prophetic gift to the Church, Gina Gholston. Pray and decree the dreams and interpretations in this incredible book, *Dreams of Awakening*. Don't simply read and be encouraged by them—they are tools! When digested and acted on, they will increase your faith, help you war, and make you successful as you build.

Enjoy!

—Dutch Sheets
Bestselling author

INTRODUCTION

Looking at the happenings in our world through the lens of natural understanding, we would undoubtedly conclude that a spiritual awakening is impossible. However, as believers, the Body of Christ, our worldview is not obstructed by the delusion, the chaos, and the fog of fear and confusion that hell has initiated. We see through the lens of God's Word and His prophetic promises.

Present throughout our history are multiple examples of how God shook nations that seemed unshakable and changed world events that seemed unchangeable. God has always had a people who believe Him; and as they humbled themselves to walk with Him in cooperation with His Spirit, through them God has time and again shown Himself strong, in spite of hell's attempts to stop or hinder His plan.

Echoing down through time are prophetic words and biblical promises that another world-shaking Great Awakening would come in a set time. That time is now. The Lord said to me, *"I Am opening a well of oath, a well of promise. I have remembered My promises. THE TIME IS NOW, and that which I have spoken will begin to bring forth the harvest of My intentions."*

God has not forgotten His promises, and He has not abandoned the Church. The Lord is with us; He is for us, and Holy Spirit is in us. Through us, He will continue to fulfill His amazing plan of the ages. The Wind is blowing again, change is happening, and awakening has begun!

This book is a compilation of many dreams, visions, and prophetic words that illustrate God's intentions to fulfill His promise of another Great Awakening in our time. Dreams, visions, and prophetic words do not, in any way, replace or take preeminence over the written Word of God, but when given by Holy Spirit, they work together with the Word as a means of instruction, insight, and revelation to help us navigate forward with wisdom and understanding that make us effective representatives and ambassadors of Christ.

We arm ourselves with the Word and with prophetic revelation so that we *"will be able to [successfully] resist and stand your ground in the evil day [of danger], and having done everything [that the crisis demands], to stand firm [in your place, fully prepared, immovable, victorious]"* (Ephesians 6:13 AMP).

It is my sincere prayer that the words, dreams, and visions that you read will spark a personal awakening inside your heart. May your heart catch the desires of God's heart and burn with a vicious hunger to draw near to Him and to be filled with the enabling power of His Spirit so that you may run with the fire and fulfill your part in His plan.

With upward focus, we are being called to take our place on the timeline of history. The wind of Holy Spirit *is* blowing again. We must be alert, stand in the wind, hold out our ember, and be ignited by the fire of God's transforming glory. Be not afraid. Be bold in the Lord and confident in His Word. Hold nothing back! The world needs what we have been given.

And *our* time...starts...now!

SECTION ONE

— 1 —

BUILDING FOR HABITATION

Now, therefore, you are no longer strangers and foreigners, but fellow citizens with the saints and members of the household of God, having been built on the foundation of the apostles and prophets, Jesus Christ Himself being the chief cornerstone, in whom the whole building, being fitted together, grows into a holy temple in the Lord, in whom you also are being built together for a dwelling place of God in the Spirit.

Ephesians 2:19-22 NKJV

One thing I most enjoy doing is visiting old home places. As I walk through the cabins, barns, and fields, it's like stepping back in time to catch a glimpse of how some families started out. There is an old adage, "Necessity is the mother of invention," and when I stroll through these homeplaces, I can see the reality of that statement. When confronted by a need, pioneers created solutions to meet it. Their determination and fortitude would not allow them to quit when there seemed to be no way to press forward.

They would find a way, and they would do whatever they had to do to survive and thrive. From building log cabins for keeping their families warm and safe, to building wagons and trains for transportation and hauling capabilities, to forging tools to build towns and cities, to developing farm equipment to be used in planting and raising crops, the innovation and determination they possessed and displayed is beyond impressive to me.

As I look at the structures and touch the tools that are still in existence today, I am always filled with appreciation for people willing to take their place in history. They gave their time, blood, sweat, and tears to carve out a life for themselves and for their families. And although they were just doing what they had to do for that moment in time, they were actually opening the way and enabling others to step into *their* place and to continue to build for *their* times.

Though primitive compared to modern-day conveniences, those early inventions and methods were actually points of origination for what would be built and done in future generations. Many people give no thought at all to these things; but the truth is, if those people had not done what they did, we would not have what we have today.

When I visit these places, I feel a connection to those times, those people. It's not that I am longing to return to those days and to try to recreate what they already did, but the legacy they left behind sparks a determination in me that provokes me to want to take my place in history.

We do a great disservice to those who have gone before us if we fail to pick up the baton that they left for us and continue to run the race. We must honor who they were and all that they did, and we do that by allowing their part to inspire us to do our part.

This is our time on the timeline; and in our time, we too must continue to build on what we have been given. Just as it was with those early pioneers, we live and do what we need to do; we build for our time. But we must keep in mind that what we do and what we build not only affects us, but our lives and our doings are leaving an inheritance for those who come after us.

Just as it is in the natural, so it is in the spiritual. In 2006, God led me to study and learn of past revivals, the great awakenings, and other powerful moves of His Spirit throughout history and even in our modern times. Until that time, I had never heard of some of these events. I was fascinated and so deeply moved by what I learned during those months of study. The testimonies of the God-happenings that I read about stirred a deep passion and desire inside me to see those things happen again!

There was a sincere appreciation and admiration that rose in me for those pioneers and revivalists who willingly took their places on the timeline of history and allowed Holy Spirit to move through them so that the testimony of Jesus and the demonstration of the power of God could impact the world around them. The sacrifices they made, the dedication of their lives unto God, and their fearless obedience to the leading of Holy Spirit allowed Heaven to invade the earth in very powerful and undeniable ways, insomuch that people were awakened to an awareness of God and began to diligently seek after Him. Entire communities, states, regions, territories, and even nations were changed as the knowledge of the glory of God burned through these devoted ones with transforming power and demonstration.

The more I read, the more I joined in the cry of Habakkuk:

> *...God, I've heard what our ancestors say about You, and I'm stopped in my tracks, down on my knees. Do among us what You did among them. Work among us as You worked among them...* (Habakkuk 3:1-2 MSG).

Christianity has a strong revival heritage that has burned through many generations. Those who have gone before us paid the price to steward the move of God in their times. Laying their reputations and even their very lives on the line, they determined to obey God so that the Gospel message could be preached and so that Christ would be made known. Because of their obedience to God, they provided future generations a foundation on which to build.

Along with the inspiration that comes with the knowledge of the transformational power of God that came as the result of those who stood devoted to God and unwilling to compromise their call to be His representatives in their time, there is also an undeniable responsibility that we must grasp so we may also allow that fire to burn in us, no matter the cost, to pass the faith along in even greater measure to those who come behind us.

The origination point for the Church is found in the second chapter of the book of Acts. The obedience of the 120 people to go and tarry in that upper room in Jerusalem positioned them to receive power from God that launched them forth as power-filled witnesses who lived and walked in the likeness of Jesus Christ. The indwelling power of Holy Spirit not only changed their own lives, He empowered them to preach the Gospel with fervency and with miracles and signs following as He reached through them to impact the whole known world with the demonstration of the reality of God.

What those apostles did in their time set the stage for the following generations to continue to run with the Gospel and to make Christ known. Since that time, the fiery river of the glory and power of God has continued to grow and flow generation after generation.

Every believer is a connection point between what was and what is to come. You may think that your part in the plan of God is not important, but every believer must understand that what we do in our time matters! What others did before us was necessary for us, and what we do now is necessary for all who come after us! We are not just building for the moment; we are also building for the future yet to be seen!

Every believer is a connection point between what was and what is to come.

So we must dare to trust God, obey Him, and demonstrate His Word. We must dare to do what He has called us to do, without fear, doubt, or hesitation, never quenching Holy Spirit and never compromising the truth! We must be determined that the legacy we leave is burning with even greater fervency than what we received.

In the year 2020 I had a dream in which God illustrated to me how the Church is continuously being built in each generation. What an amazing dream it was! I share it with you now:

> I was with a group of people, including apostle and teacher Dutch Sheets, apostolic prophet Chuck Pierce, and other people I know. In the dream, because of the look of the buildings and the way the people around us were dressed, it seemed to me we were in an early American, colonial

days' setting and time. There were many people scurrying around, all very busy working.

A lady wearing some type of bonnet and a long cotton dress came up to us. Her dress was made of very thick off-white material with a full white apron atop. She excitedly said to us, "We've been waiting for you! Now, I must show you what is happening."

We then went into an area where there was a very, very large building that was in the process of being built. The building's walls were being built with handmade bricks, but the foundation was made of very old stones.

Pointing toward this building, the lady said to us, "This is the foundation of America's hope." In that moment, our entire group felt the presence of Holy Spirit, and I asked the lady, "What *is* this building?"

She replied with such reverence, almost in a whisper, "This is none other than the House of God. These stones are the ancient stones of the foundation that was laid, and EVERY generation MUST build on this foundation."

As we moved closer to the building, we could see that it was being built upward from the foundation. There were levels that went up to a certain point, and then another level would start and go higher. There were several levels in the walls of the building, which were all made of handmade bricks; but in each level, we could tell a difference in the materials used to make the bricks.

The lady then said to us, "Each of these levels represents generations that have built their part."

All of the work happening around us was revealing to us the colonial generation as they were building their part onto the House of God. People were working on different tasks. Some men with horses were hammering horseshoes on an anvil. Others were forging and hammering out tools. Some were making bricks. Some were very reverently placing the bricks on the walls of the building.

Some ladies were washing garments in large black, cast-iron kettles sitting on fires to boil the water. The lady in the long dress said to us, "These types of things have to be done in every generation." Then she pointed to the ladies at the kettles, and she said, "The garments *must* be washed and cleaned."

Then she drew our attention to the workers adding bricks to the building, and said, "The House of God has had to be repaired and restored in many generations." (I knew she meant that some generations had failed to do their part, leaving the following generation to have to repair and restore what was left undone, as well as to carry on with their part.)

Beside the lady was a man sitting in a chair in front of a desk. He was typing on something that looked like a stenotype machine. I approached him and asked, "What are you doing?"

He said, "I am calculating the timing for your generation—the moment when it will be *your* turn to build and do your part for the House of God." As he typed, the paper he was typing on was rolling out of the machine, and there came a moment when he finished typing. He tore the paper from the machine and carefully rolled it up and gave it to Dutch Sheets, and he said to Dutch, "You will know when the time has come!"

Then the man who had been typing and the lady who had been speaking began to lead us into this House of God. As we walked up the steps, she pointed to the foundation of the building and said, "This is the foundation on which America MUST be built."

I could see that the words of Ephesians 2:19-22 were carved into the cornerstone:

> *Now, therefore, you are no longer strangers and foreigners, but fellow citizens with the saints and members of the household of God, having been built on the foundation of the apostles and prophets, Jesus Christ Himself being the chief cornerstone, in whom the whole building, being fitted together, grows into a holy temple in the Lord, in whom you also are being built together for a dwelling place of God in the Spirit* (Ephesians 2:19-22 NKJV).

In the dream, I was struck by the realization that these people were the colonists, the ones who founded what would become known as the United States of America. They knew the importance and necessity of building it on that foundation.

As we entered the building, we all felt the presence of God so strongly. During our time inside this building, there were moments that were so full of His weighty presence that none of us could stand—at other times that weighty glory would wane, and though His presence was still felt, it wasn't as strong. This pattern continued the entire time we were inside the building. I asked the man and woman why that was, and the old man said, "Every generation experiences a move of God, some at greater degrees than others. But every generation is given the assignment of building more and more onto the House of God.

However, most just get caught up in the excitement of the movement and fail to build for the next generation, and the glory that was experienced in their times will wane and will have to be reignited in the next generation. But the embers of those moves are always caught and carried by some, and the wind will blow again and reignite the embers. Many people, in each generation, can only see their part, and they think that's all there is, but that's *not* all there is. The move of God comes, not only for the moment, but to empower them to continue to build on the foundation. They must do their part so the next generation can do their part."

We then made our way out of the building, and once outside, we stopped. It was as if we were on a slow-moving train; however, we were not really moving at all. We were watching times pass before us. It was like we were watching a movie. We saw the time periods of the 1800s, into the early 1900s, and to the mid-1900s. In each of these time periods, we saw people doing the same types of things that we had just witnessed in the colonial setting.

As this "movie" was playing out before us, we heard and saw a huge wind come into the House of God, and a massive fire was reignited in each of those time periods. With great force, fire shot out from the building into the nation. As we watched this passing-of-time movie, the flame and the wind would die down some, and then the wind would blow again, and the fire would reignite.

We all somehow knew this was depicting the Second Great Awakening in America, the frontier revivals, Azusa Street, the healing revivals, and other moves of God that occurred during those specific years. And though the movements would come and then die down, we could see that much was built onto the House of God during those times.

We also realized that this is what we had felt when we had been inside the building and the weighty glory of God would come and then wane. We had experienced the glory of God as it had moved through the generations.

And then everything went silent. That's when the man told Dutch to unroll the paper that he had given to him earlier. As Dutch unrolled the paper, we saw written at the top was "Ezra 9:8-9." Although I only saw the reference, the Scripture reads:

> *And now for a little while grace has been shown from the Lord our God, to leave us a remnant to escape, and to give us a peg in His holy place, that our God may enlighten our eyes and give us a measure of revival in our bondage. For we were slaves. Yet our God did not forsake us in our bondage; but He extended mercy to us in the sight of the*

> *kings of Persia, to revive us, to repair the house of our God, to rebuild its ruins, and to give us a wall in Judah and Jerusalem* (Ezra 9:8-9 NKJV).

As this was happening, we felt a wind stirring around us. The lady then very excitedly said, "The wind is blowing again! Hold out the embers that you carry! Let them be reignited in the wind, but don't just rejoice in the movement that is coming. It's your time to build *your* part onto the House of God!"

The wind was getting stronger, and we each reached inside ourselves somehow and pulled out an ember. We held the ember out in front of us, and the wind was quickly reigniting it. It was burning hot in our hands, but we held it, determined not to let it fall to the ground.

Then some of the women who had been washing the garments came over to each of us, and like seamstresses with measuring tapes they began to measure us. I asked the lady in the long dress what was happening, and she said to us, "You are each being fitted for the garments you will wear in the days to come." Then she calmly said, "And *your* time... starts...now."

That's all I remember of the dream.

IT'S TIME TO REKINDLE THE FIRE

In reading about all the past moves of God, I found a familiar thread woven through each one—the thread of the awareness of His undeniable presence.

"Wherever you went you could not get away from the presence of the Lord."

"God was everywhere, in the very atmosphere. Whether they were godly or godless, people knew that God was there."

"There was an increasing consciousness of God's presence."

These are only a few statements made by those who experienced those true revivals. These revivals transformed culture and impacted generations years beyond their time as the continuation of the fire of God blazed its way throughout time, marking each generation with the glory of His presence and shouting a witness of the reality of Jesus, the power of God, and the operation of Holy Spirit for those who would follow.

The fire of God symbolizes several things to me—His demonstrated power, unstoppable movement, and His undeniable presence. But perhaps the most important revelation of the fire of God is His transforming glory. To encounter the all-consuming Fire Himself, is to be changed and transformed. This is how I visualize awakening: God comes, and in *His* presence everything changes.

Our Christian heritage is one of power, fire, and the demonstration of the glory of God that transforms lives, society, and culture. One of the saddest things I have witnessed in my lifetime is the obvious decline of true faith, godliness, and devotion to God in the Church. Too many Christians have sat hidden inside church walls, shrouded in titles and lifeless forms, leaning more and more to conformity and compromise, while the demonstration of the power of God has become less and less. Slowly, the fire of God's presence has been replaced by compromise that stemmed from the deception that we had to become more like the world to be more "acceptable" to society.

Devotion and purity have been replaced with a watered-down version of truth. Many within the Church have become comfortable and have learned to live without the fervency of the fire of the presence of God and without fresh vision for going beyond where we have been and what we have known. Instead of fearless, faith-filled pioneers who kept moving more and more into the deeper things of God, many became settlers who were unwilling to embrace the call to surrender all, so that the fullness of Christ could be experienced and revealed.

TRUE RIGHTEOUSNESS

Abandoning true righteousness, many created their own form of righteousness that may have been palatable to a godless society, but it has been void of the true power of God. Now we find ourselves surrounded by the effects of a generation that has been raised without the influence, knowledge, and demonstration of the Word, the power, and the fire of God! And in the absence of truth and in the decline of the manifested presence of God among us, entire generations are vulnerable and easily ensnared by the blinding darkness of the god of this world!

Somehow many in the Church began to convince themselves that we didn't need all of that "old stuff." They failed to take the baton and run the race that was set before them. Some have neglected the most important things, and the fire of God's presence and the light of continuous revelation began to wane, leaving them to believe that our wisdom, talents, technology, and skills would be enough to sustain us—that it would be the best way to draw people in to hear the Gospel message. While wisdom, talents, technology, and skills can be beneficial tools for advancing the Kingdom of God, they are by no means a sufficient substitute for the glory and fire of God.

We can have all of the "cool" features that will attract the world to our buildings, but if people are not confronted by truth and demonstration of the Spirit of God when they come, there can and will be no lasting change impacting our culture. And if we are not tending the fire—keeping Jesus as the central focus and His presence our number one priority—we are merely living a lifeless, visionless existence, passing down a powerless form that will be replicated by those who follow our example!

We MUST have *Him!* It's time for the leaders to discover the fortitude of those who have gone before us, and with undaunted resolve, once again rise and run with the flame to stoke up the fires of our Pentecostal inheritance!

Only God can bring real change to lives that are lost and broken. Only Jesus can connect us to God; and only by the manifestation of the Spirit and power will we see nations transformed and hearts turned back to God. Cultural transformation, multiple salvations through acceptance of Jesus as Lord, deliverance, healing—these are some of the fruits of a true awakening to God ignited by the allowing and acceptance of the fire of His holy presence.

God never called the Church to "fit in" to the culture. As a matter of fact, He calls us to *"shine as lights"* in the *"midst of a crooked and perverse generation"* (Philippians 2:15 NKJV). Jesus said, *"You are the light of the world. ...let your light shine before others, that they may see your good works and glorify your Father in Heaven"* (Matthew 5:14,16 NIV). And Moses reveals that the only thing that makes us stand out, shine as lights, and sets us apart in the world is God's presence (see Exodus 33:15-16). We *must* have the fire of His presence!

THE FIRE OF GOD

The fire of God marks us. It reveals God's power through us. The glory residue that lingered on Moses after he encountered the God of fire was so powerful that he had to cover his face just so people could look at him (see Exodus 34:35). God is powerful; and when He is present, His power transforms us and shines through us in unmistakable ways. God's desire is to fill us with His Spirit, burn in us with His fire, and shine His light through us so that we can know Him and also make Him known to the world around us.

God told the priests who attended to the altar of the Tabernacle that the fire must always be burning and must never go out (see Leviticus 6:13). In Leviticus 9:24 (NIV) we read:

> *Fire came out from the presence of the Lord and consumed the burnt offering and the fat portions on the altar. And when all the people saw it, they shouted for joy and fell facedown.*

We see in these Scriptures that the reason the continuation of the fire is so important to God is because it was started directly by God, Himself. It came out from His presence, and He commanded the priests to maintain and keep fervent what He had started.

As the fire came out from the presence of the Lord, there was a visible and powerful demonstration as it consumed the burnt offering. That demonstration captured the attention of the people who saw it, and the response was one of reverence and awe of God. Those people were impacted by what they saw, and what they saw was the result of the priests doing their part in keeping the fire of God burning.

The good work that God has begun in the Church came out of Him, and His intentions are that we steward well and keep fervent what He has begun in us. And the degree of fervency released through our lives, our ministries, and our churches is determined by the proximity of His presence. He is the fire, and the closer we come to Him, the closer He comes to us. And where He is, there is power and fire that will capture the attention of those around us.

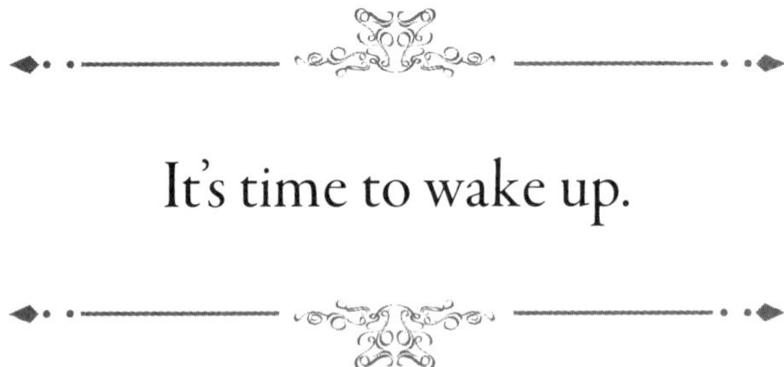

It's time to wake up.

The Church began in the fire and demonstration of the presence of God (see Acts, chapter 2), and we must never allow that fire to go out. Though it has seemed to dwindle, the wind is blowing, and the fire is beginning to burn again. There is a stirring, a shaking, an awakening happening. The Lord said to my friend, Tim Sheets, "The alarm clock of Heaven is now ringing on the nightstand of a sleeping church. It's time to rise. It's time to rise to the occasion. It's time to get up!"

I heard the Spirit of the Lord say,

The wind is blowing! Hear it in the Spirit and know that I will blow My breath into this nation—resurrection and Pentecost, all rolled up into one unprecedented move of My Spirit. It will be an undeniable, gushing blast of the wind of My Spirit. It will not be a momentary stirring, but a transforming habitation of My fiery glory, My manifested presence.

God has not forgotten the seeds of prophetic promises that He sowed into the Church in the book of Acts. He has not forgotten the seeds of prophetic promises that He has spoken concerning this nation. He has not forgotten the seeds of prophetic promises He has spoken concerning you—and He has not forgotten one word He spoke through those pioneers and revivalists of days gone by concerning another Great Awakening that would unfold in our time! He remembers and declares, *"My covenant I will not break, nor alter the word that has gone out of My lips"* (Psalm 89:34 NKJV). Those seeds have been waiting for their moment, and this is that moment. Awakening has begun.

Hear and receive this word from the Lord:

If you will allow Me to do it and if you will receive it, I will remove all doubts and fears concerning the vision I gave to you. I Am reaffirming and strongly reasserting My Word to you so as to re-secure its root lest you forget, grow weary, and fail to move with Me in this season!

I will awaken you in the night seasons with dreams and visions, and you will remember My Word, My vision—even things I have spoken to you that you have forgotten. I Am jolting your memory; and as you remember, joy, excitement, and expectation will be restored as it was when I very first spoke to you concerning these things...because now is the time!

> *I have not forgotten! I Am remembering even now the path that I set you on, even in your youth! I Am restoring to you the remembrance of that old path, and I Am reigniting the joy and fervency of your pursuit of Me! It is time, and I Am culminating the years, the events, the words, the visions, the dreams, the obedience, and the steps you have taken. I Am pulling it all together, and soon you will see My purpose in it all!*
>
> *Do not lose heart and do not grow weary, not now! Not ever! Stay focused on Me so I can show you how it all shall unfold, and so I can launch you forward—focused, prepared, and free from confining limitations! Hoist your sails. My wind is beginning to blow!*

Recently I heard the Lord say,

> *There is a rekindling of an "old flame"—a fire you thought had died out. I Am blowing on the embers even now! Revival fire is here! I Am rekindling and reigniting the flame! I will burn, and you will see it! I will burn, and many will be drawn to the fire of My presence. Watch Me burn again among and through My people, giving light and demonstration of the working of My power.*

We must never look back at what God has done as though God *is* done! Paul, speaking of the things written in the Scriptures, said, *"For whatever things were written before were written for our learning..."* (Romans 15:4 NKJV). What God has done in the past was amazing, and it is so encouraging to look back to learn and to hear of those mighty acts, but we must never do so with the belief that that's all there is. He is not finished! He's just getting started. Those things advanced God's purposes in *that* time, and they also serve as a witness to us *today*. As we read of those accounts, God speaks through them to declare to us,

> *What I have done, I will do again, and even greater. Don't try to recreate that, but do learn from it. To have what they had, do what they did, but don't stop there. Advance with the fervency of My awakening fires in your time!*

The wind is blowing, reigniting the fire, and the knowledge of the glory will once again cover the earth as the waters cover the sea. Will you be one of the faithful who carries and burns with the fire? I have always been impacted by this amazing quote by Jim Elliot:

> He makes His ministers a flame of fire. Am I ignitable? God deliver me from the dread asbestos of "other things." Saturate me with the oil of the Spirit that I may be a flame. Make me Thy fuel, Flame of God.[1]

May this be our sincere prayer as we take our place on the timeline of history: "Make us Your flame, O God!" May our generation shout to the next generation the goodness of God, not just with words, but with power and demonstration of the undeniable works of the Spirit of God.

REOPENING THE WELLS OF REVIVAL

Powerful moves of God have taken place that had supernatural spiritual impact that transformed lives, governments, cultures, and nations. Knowledge of those moves of God should not just leave us in awe of what God did, but should inspire and provoke us to believe that what God has done, He can and will do again! Those revivals are not just past history. They are the headwaters of rivers of living waters that flow with an unstoppable current of glory and power! And we have entered the time when God is reopening the wells to release the waters of undeniable awakening again in our time.

There is power in the current, and there is fire on those rivers—the fire of God that blazed throughout history, giving humankind true experience and encounters with the living God! Those fires must be kept burning, increasing with greater and greater fervency in each generation. It is God's commandment that, *"The fire must be kept burning on the altar continuously; it must not go out"* (Leviticus 6:13 NIV). God is uncapping the wells, and He is stoking the flames to spearhead another greater move in our time because it's time. Awakening has begun!

OUR PART

What does that mean for you and me? Do we just sit around and wait for an emotional experience in our church gatherings and conferences? Those times of refreshing are great, but is that all there is to a move of God?

Awakening is the result of a confrontation with the reality and holiness of God.

I believe for many in the Church, their idea of revival and awakening is that the glory of God is going to come to a church through a preacher, and everybody is going to go to that church and listen to that preacher, sit around the fire, and enjoy the momentary touch. Their idea of revival is that a few meetings will take place where everyone is "zapped" by some emotional manifestations, but eventually the fervency will wane, and we will all just go back to the way it's always been. They view revival as a fleeting celebration that just comes and goes, and doesn't cost us anything. But that is not what true awakening is going to look like.

Awakening is the result of a confrontation with the reality and holiness of God. As we become more aware of Him, as the old song says, "the things of earth will grow strangely dim, in the light of His glory and grace."[2] A spark is ignited inside that brings us to an awakened realization that He is all we want and all we need. That realization sets us on a path of unrelenting pursuit of greater understanding and knowledge of Him. We shake off the conformities of this world and turn our worship and focus back onto God and Jesus.

As we draw near to God, He draws near to us; and in the place of His abiding presence, we experience more than just emotional gratification. We hear Him. We feel His heart, we receive strategies to accomplish His purposes, we become carriers of the fire of God and witnesses of His glory. We are changed and equipped to show forth the reality of Jesus in such a way that not only are our church services impacted, but society, culture, territories, and even nations are impacted by the power of God released through us to touch people's lives, thus awakening *them* to the knowledge of God that leads them to salvation.

One of the ways that God is bringing awakening to the Church today is through dreams and visions. I, along with many others, have received such detailed dreams about revival and awakening that we have to conclude these are not just random dreams. They are actually prophetic revelations. If we allow Holy Spirit to give us insight, we can receive strategy and understanding for where we are, how to move forward, and how to rightly discern what God is doing in the earth right now.

The dreams included in section one of this book give illustrations that help us see and understand the impact of true revival and awakening.

Notes

1. Elisabeth Elliot, *Shadow of the Almighty: The Life and Testament of Jim Elliot* (San Francisco, CA: HarperCollins, 1979).
2. Helen H. Lemmel, "Turn Your Eyes upon Jesus," 1922.

— 2 —

THE SPEARHEAD IS FORMING

Revive us again, O God! I know You will! Give us a fresh start! Then all Your people will taste Your joy and gladness.

Psalm 85:6 TPT

History records a move of God that took place in 1800 just south of Russellville, Kentucky, near the Red River. In that year, a group of about twenty people met for several weeks to make an appeal to Heaven for revival to come to that frontier land, which was filled with crime, outlaws, and ungodliness.

In response to that sincere appeal, Heaven came down in a very powerful way, and the hearts of the most hardened men and women were undeniably transformed by supernatural encounters with God that they experienced during that camp meeting revival. The revival changed the atmosphere of the entire region, and historians say it actually sparked the Second Great Awakening in our nation.

If you travel there today, you will find situated in the shade of multiple black walnut trees a simple log structure that is a replica of the actual building that once echoed with travailing prayers prayed by hungry and devoted saints of God, with fiery proclamations of the Gospel message, and with shouts of jubilation as people experienced the presence and life-changing power and love of Christ. I have been to this location many times to pray and have found that there is a residue of the glory of God that still lingers there. There is also a deep awareness in the Spirit that can be felt, which gives a knowing that the water from that well is still available.

The following dream reveals God's heart and intentions to uncap this and other wells of revival—not a re-creation of those moves of God, but rather a releasing of the genuine flow of an unstoppable outpouring of His glory again in our time.

> In the dream, I was standing on the grounds of the Red River Meeting House. I had gone through the gate and started walking up the driveway toward the log structure. In front of me, in the dip as I went up to the building, I noticed that there were one hundred bald eagles, standing on the ground. For a moment, my complete focus was captivated by the sight of all those eagles.
>
> Then hearing a noise behind me, I turned and saw an older well-drilling rig coming through the gate toward the Meeting House. It stopped about halfway up the driveway, and backed up toward the log structure, stopping under the walnut trees. Those in the truck got out and began the process of lowering the large bit to begin drilling. No sooner had the bit touched the ground when *whoosh,* the water came gushing out! It was shooting up very high into the air in massive amounts!
>
> I thought, *This looks like Old Faithful.* I have seen that geyser and this scene made me think of it—only this flow was MUCH larger! I was thinking about how Old Faithful

is very predictable and that it gushes forth in a rhythm of time. Then I heard an audible voice in the dream, speaking about this geyser in front of me, saying, "It is set on the rhythm of Heaven's time clock. It's time!" I understood that to mean, "It's blown before, a gushing move of the Spirit of God, but it's set for another, greater gusher, and it's time!"

Next, I saw two hands come down and clap once. The clap made a very loud sound that was a signal to the eagles. When they heard the clap, the eagles rose up, hovering, ready to fly. They weren't scared by the noise of the clap or by the spraying of the water. They just simultaneously rose and calmly hovered.

When they started rising up, I saw that each eagle had in one of their talons some arrows, and in their other talon they had a rolled-up piece of paper. When they rose up, hovering, I then heard the audible voice speak again, saying, "Rapid eye movement: My seers are on the move." As soon as I heard those words, the eagles flew off in every direction. It wasn't a random flight; it was as though each one was on an assignment, heading purposely in the direction they were sent to carry out those assignments.

As they left the Red River Meeting House area, each eagle flew through the gushing water, was soaked with the water, and they carried it with them. The water never dried off them. Wherever they went, as they flew, the geyser water fell off them like a rain shower onto the dry ground below.

The water was still gushing, and I too was soaked with it. I went into the Meeting House, and it was set up like a command center. There were seven drafting tables with "architects" sitting at them, drawing up blueprints or plans. People were coming in, one right after the other, soaked in the water from the gusher. Each person approached one of the architects who was drawing up the blueprints. The architects would then tear off the blueprint, roll it up, and then hand it to the person.

It's hard to explain, but immediately after rolling up one page, the architects would very rapidly draw another blueprint for the next person who approached. I was amazed by the speed with which the architects worked! They would draw the blueprint, roll it up, and hand it off; draw it, roll it up, and hand it off. This was happening over and over *very, very* quickly!

I then noticed there were pipes built into the walls of the Red River Meeting House. I knew these pipes went out of the building in every direction. When the people received the paper, the architect would point them in the direction of one of the pipes. The person would then get into their appointed pipe to be "sent" where they needed to go with those blueprints.

In the dream, I thought, *This is like sending email.* I thought of fiber optics. I knew that just like it is with an email, these people were getting into the pipes and being "sent," along with the blueprints, to wherever in the nation or the world they were needed. As soon as they got in the pipes, *whoosh*, they instantly arrived at their destinations with the blueprints. These people were soaked with the water from the gushing well, and it was raining off them like it did from the eagles!

Then I heard that same audible voice say, "Rapid response teams." I looked up, and on the wall behind the pulpit in the meeting house I saw a sign that read, "Rapid Response Command Center."

Then the dream shifted. I suddenly, somehow knew that what was happening at the Red River Meeting House was also happening at Cane Ridge, Kentucky, and it was happening at Azusa Street in California too.

I was then lifted up and could see a drawing of a line connecting Cane Ridge, Kentucky and the Red River Meeting House. Going out from Cane Ridge and from the Red River Meeting House were other lines—one from each of them—going to and connecting at Azusa Street. As I was lifted high above the nation, I could see that these lines formed the shape of a spearhead. And from the center of the line that was drawn between Cane Ridge and the Red River Meeting House was another line. I knew that this line came from the nation of Wales, and it had formed the "shaft" of the "spear."

It was a drawing depicting that all four of those places—Wales, Cane Ridge, Red River Meeting House, and Azusa Street—were connected, and what I saw happening at Red River was simultaneously happening in those other places too. I knew I was being shown that the culmination of all those past moves of God were now being brought together to "spearhead" another greater and more powerful move of God in our time.

And that was the end of the dream.

Red River Meeting House, Cane Ridge, Azusa Street, and Wales are places where revival fires once burned. The full historical significance of each of these revivals is truly worth your time to research. The deep impact each of these revivals had on lives, societies, and nations during their times is beyond description. And the deep impact each had and continues to have on lives, societies, and even nations beyond their times is undeniable.

However, as powerful as each of these revivals were, God is revealing through this dream, that He is now culminating those anointings to "spearhead" another greater move of His Spirit in our time. These revival wells are bulging and are now being reopened to release the flow of awakening. What God has done in the past is not lost nor forgotten. He has a set time for the release of what has been preserved and reserved—and this is that time!

I believe this dream is a clear picture of the appropriate posture of the Body of Christ in anticipation of awakening. We are not to be just sitting around waiting to "feel" something. We believe God. We believe His prophets. We believe His Word, and we must allow what God has said and continues to say to affect our prayers, lives, ministries, the way we "do" church, and the way we see what is happening around us.

We are not focused on and driven by the way things appear. We set ourselves in agreement with God; therefore, we are able to listen for, hear, and obey His voice. We pray with expectation and unquenchable anticipation for the release of His river to create a movement that will provoke an unstoppable awakening to an awareness of God that covers the earth as the waters cover the sea.

We are convinced that as those wells are being opened, the flow will come, not just *to* the Church, but *in* us and *through* us. There is an understanding in the hearts of those positioned that the destiny on which we are embarking is not just a free ride on a fleeting wave; it's a total commitment to God to allow the torrential river of His glory to flow into us to transform us so it can flow out through us with power to bring supernatural change. We are expecting and willing to be filled with the full effects of this revival river so we can be empowered to move with its flow. We position ourselves to listen for His sound and to receive His assignments so we can carry what we receive to the places where we are sent.

Total commitment to God allows His glory to flow into us, transforming us with power to bring supernatural change in people and places.

In the dream, the eagles represent to me the "seers," those who see in the Spirit—prophets, intercessors, prophetic dreamers, and the like. These seers are now positioned to hear a sound, a signal that is provoking movement. They are prepared to go forth with rolled-up pieces of paper (strategies) and arrows as part of initiating national and even worldwide release of the waters and fires of revival.

The rising of the eagles came first in the dream. I believe it is vitally important for the seers to see and respond to the leading of Holy Spirit. The "rapid eye movement" made way for the "rapid response teams" to get in the place where they could receive the blueprints, or assignments, from the architects. These architects were receiving and effectively revealing the necessary assignments for each person, and equipping and sending them forth as carriers of the glory and carriers of the waters of awakening revival to the nation and to the nations of the world. This is a picture of the necessary function of the Church.

There are assignments that God is ready to impart to us. Be alert in the Spirit, and be receptive as Holy Spirit orders your steps. These assignments may have to do with prayer initiatives, ministry opportunities, business opportunities, prophetic prayer journeys, ideas, concepts, insights, whatever the case may be. And regardless where the assignment leads us or what the assignment requires of us, we must be ready to go with keen vision and the strength of Jehovah to fulfill those purposes.

The attention of the eagles, the sudden bursting forth of the geyser, and the readiness of the rapid response teams all point us to the need to be aware, awake, and ready to move quickly. We must allow God to deal with any and all things that could possibly hinder our forward advancement. Someone once said, "If you have to get ready, you're not ready," so now is the time to lay aside any weight and sin that could easily slow you down. Launching time is here, and we must BE ready to respond at a moment's notice.

You can feel the momentum building as the curtain is lifted to reveal the stage of this major defining moment. If we yield ourselves in full devotion to the Lord, allowing Him to do in us whatever He needs to do to free us for the launching, we will step onto the stage as a prepared people, moving into a prepared moment to accomplish the fulfillment of a prepared destiny.

"If you have to get ready, you're not ready."

Pray with me:

Father, we set our expectation above what we can think or imagine. We refuse to allow our human understanding to confine us to the limitations of our human capabilities. We will move with You, empowered by Your Holy Spirit to hear and do all You desire to show and accomplish.

We believe that which is "set" to the rhythm of Heaven's time clock has intersected its moment—and it's time! Father, give us ears to hear with clarity and give us eyes to see with precision and accuracy so we may align with Your plan and move in time with Your will and intentions.

We commit ourselves to listen and to move quickly in response to Your sending. Like Jesus, we will say what You tell us to say, go where You tell us to go, and do what You tell us to do as You bring us into the timing of the culmination of all the past moves of Your Spirit that forms the spearhead of this even greater move of Yours in our times.

The waters of the wells of revival are being opened. Father, drench us in those revival waters. Saturate us with Your Spirit. May Your reviving waters flow in us to transform us into the likeness of Christ, and may His power and love flow out through us everywhere we go, bringing life and quenching the thirst of those who cry out for the Living Water—Jesus.

We step into this move with a readiness to receive Your strategies. We set ourselves to listen for Your clarion call. We listen for Your sound, and we will move in alignment with You. You order our steps, and we will step where You order to carry out the assignments and purposes that You have planned for us in this time. We commit ourselves completely to You, and we will go as Christ's ambassadors to carry out Your will and intentions. We know and believe that You will empower us by Your Spirit to fulfill every assignment. Your angels accompany us and work on our behalf to assist us in these endeavors.

Your plan of the ages will be fulfilled, and we take our place to do our part in that plan. All for Your glory!

In Jesus' name.

Amen!

— 3 —

IGNITING THE SATURATED BUNDLES

Arise, shine; For your light has come! And the glory of the Lord is rise upon you. For behold, the darkness shall cover the earth, and deep darkness the people; but the Lord will arise over you, and His glory will be seen upon you.

Isaiah 60:1, 2 NKJV

In another dream:

> I was at Pastor John Kilpatrick's church in Alabama. (I have never been to his church, but in the dream, I knew that's where I was.) I was walking down a hallway, and I sat down for a moment in the foyer. Through the passing crowd of people, I could see a door that was opened to the sound booth. Inside the sound booth, I could see Pastor Kilpatrick sitting on a seat, talking with the sound technician. At that moment, he looked out and saw me, and motioned for me to come into that room. I walked over and went into the sound booth, and he said to me, "I know you, don't I?"

I said, "Yes," and I reminded him that we had ministered together in a church a few years prior.

He said, "Yes, I remember you. I thought I recognized you."

Then the scene changed, and we were inside the sanctuary. The meeting had started, and it was very crowded. I heard Pastor John Kilpatrick's voice coming through the sound system saying, "Where's that girl from Tennessee? Come up here!" Reluctantly, I went up onto the stage. Pastor Kilpatrick stood to the left of me. He handed me the microphone. I was very nervous, but I lifted the microphone and began to speak. I was not facing the congregation; I was looking at Pastor Kilpatrick.

Suddenly Holy Spirit encompassed me, and out of my mouth calmly came these four words, "The wind is blowing." As those words left my mouth, the Spirit of God moved upon Pastor Kilpatrick, and he fell to the floor under the power of God.

I then turned to the congregation, and pointing toward Pastor Kilpatrick, under a strong anointing, I began to prophesy, "What was will be again, but it will be different this time. This time it will not be a million people coming to one place to find Me. This time there are 'bundles' of people, who are saturated with My Spirit, who will come into places where My fire is present, and they will be touched by the fire and be immediately ignited with My glory. They will then carry that fire with them as they go. They will come in contact with other 'bundles' of people who are saturated with the oil of My Spirit, and they, too, will catch the fire and carry it and spread it to other 'bundles.' This is what awakening will look like. This is how My glory will spread to the nation and to the nations of the world."

And that was the end of the dream.

To me, Pastor John Kilpatrick represents revival. When I awoke from the dream, the Lord immediately spoke to me saying, *"Revival has remembered and recognized you and is giving you a platform to release My wind that will fan into flames, My fire that will ignite My saturated ones. Those who are saturated with the oil of My Spirit will quickly catch and carry the fire, and it will spread across this nation and into the nations of the world like wildfire on dry grass!"*

The time has come when the prophesied awakening is upon us, and revival is the platform. The platform of which God spoke was not referring to a physical structure or a stage, but rather a standard, a basis, a proclamation that will set the tone for the future movement of the Body of Christ. Revival is the message of this hour, and as leaders and ministers begin to proclaim the message, an expectation will be ignited within the Body of Christ. The platforms of ministry will no longer be about us. Church will no longer be about our coming together for a ritualistic gathering that may, at best, create a momentary, emotional touch but does not set an atmosphere where people can experience a life-changing encounter with God.

The wind of the Spirit is blowing to once again stoke the flames of revival. God once said to me that He speaks *"with intent to perform."* What He has spoken, He will do in His set time. He has spoken through His prophets of another Great Awakening coming in our time, and those prophecies have come into the moment of their prophetic timing!

DESTINY AND TIMING

Destiny and timing have now met to release the clarion sound that initiates revival—a restoration of the knowledge of Christ to capture the attention of people, awakening them to an awareness of Christ and their need for Him as Savior and Lord. As Christ once again becomes the central focus of the Church, the demonstration of the power and of the Spirit will be revealed. He will be seen, and lives will be transformed as we encounter the magnificence of His glory.

Revival is glory revealed.

Revival will not just be about a few consecutive nights where we gather in a building for some preplanned "services."

Revival is:

- Glory revealed
- Putting our focus back on Jesus
- Restoration of life
- Undeniable power demonstrated to bring undeniable change

- An awakening alarm to those who have been lulled to sleep by the deceiving tones of a godless culture
- Restoration of consciousness

This is the platform. This is the message: Christ is in us, working through us with power to shift the spiritual climate of nations. Through us, He is bringing an awareness of the reality of God with the brilliance of the light of His glory that destroys the power of the blinding darkness that has captivated the hearts and minds of so many, freeing them to see God and receive Christ as their Savior.

The dream wasn't just about Pastor Kilpatrick and me; it was about revival and awakening. It was about honor and purpose. It was an announcement that what is unfolding now is greater and more far-reaching than we can even imagine with our natural understanding.

The wind of God will fan the flames of revival, igniting those who are ignitable. God has a remnant of people who have refused to settle for mundane religiosity. This remnant is not gauging this present move by how God used to move. They honor what God has done, but they know there is more—and they feel it is time for the revealing of the more!

Just as the eagles in the Red River Meeting House dream and the saturated "bundles" in this dream, this remnant company is positioned in anticipation for the sound of awakening. That sound is now ringing with an unmistakable signal that is announcing, "It's time!" It's time to rise, and we rise! We shake off lethargy and compromise, and we rise with courageous faith to receive and obey the assignments to be carried beyond the walls of our churches and even beyond the perimeters of the previous moves of God. We go beyond!

Revival is not about just one geographical location where a move of God happens and everyone descends on that place to get a touch from

God. It's more than that! I *do* believe that there will be specific places that will be ignited to burn with the fire of God's demonstrated presence, but it will not be for the purpose of drawing a crowd to a building, nor will it be about a preacher becoming famous and gathering a following. Revival is not about our glory and fame—it's all about *His* glory and *His* fame being made known to and through His Body. If we embrace this truth, surrender our lives and platforms for the proclamation of *His* platform, we will be aligned with His purposes, working with Him in the unfolding of His plan.

WATERS FOR A DRY LAND

We celebrate and honor the historic happenings experienced in the past moves of God, but we must never forget that those moves were stewarded by believers who hungered for the *real* of God. They humbled themselves before Him to walk with Him and to be willing vessels through whom He could work. They availed themselves wholly to God and allowed Him to guide them. Guide them He did, and obediently they followed, regardless of the cost! Their unquenchable desire to experience more of Him birthed fervent intercession and obedience to God that would not relent until whole atmospheres were saturated by the waters of His glory.

They dedicated their time and their lives to Christ and for His righteous cause. Relentless intercession became the consistent posture. "Bend us!" they cried. "Pour out Your water on the dry land," they pleaded. "God, we will give You no rest until You come," they dared to proclaim. And transformation came as rivers of His fiery water flowed through them in unstoppable currents that opened the way for others to see Christ and to experience the reality of His power and Person.

The reopening of those wells of revival requires a return to that kind of sold-out devotion to Christ. It requires that we allow the Potter to reshape us until Christ be formed in us and His Spirit fills us and His fire marks us—not just with words, but with *power* and *demonstration* of His Spirit. As we devote ourselves to Him in prayer and obedience, believing His Word, believing the true prophets, praying in the Holy Spirit, we are being saturated with the oil of His presence, becoming fuel for the flame of God!

As mentioned previously, I believe some specific places will be ignited with the fires of revival, and some specific ministers will be called of God to preach the revival message. The saturated ones will come to these places, hear the message, and be touched by the fire. But the encounter they experience in these places will not be about a momentary touch that will fade away when they leave the building.

This is lasting, lingering power, producing total transformation as they encounter the God of fire, and He marks them with His glory. They will not only be touched by the fire, they will be filled with the fire, and they will carry it everywhere they go. They will be an ignition point for other saturated believers who may never step through the doors of the places where the fire originated. This is what awakening looks like.

God is not coming just to visit with us—He's coming to inhabit us so that through us He can be made known to the world around us. Revival has recognized us. We are the generation who will seek God. We seek His face. We seek His fullness. We are no longer satisfied with mundane. Revival is our platform, and our proclamation is now:

> *Lift up your heads, O you gates! And be lifted up, you everlasting doors! And the King of glory shall come in. Who is the King of glory? The Lord strong and mighty, the Lord mighty in battle* (Psalm 24:7-8 NKJV).

Pray with me:

Father, take us to a deeper place in You, beyond the surface of all the stuff we've made You to be. Take us to a deeper place in You that produces the fire in us that we have yet to know but must know if we are to be part of the company that advances forward with You in this time!

Take us beyond the surface. Take us beyond that manageable form that has appeased our comfort levels, the form that produces just enough to say You are near, but does not provoke the full surrender that happens when You are here!

May we be touched by the fire of Your glory, and may that touch cause us to abandon our comfort to pursue the depths of You that causes us to lose ourselves in Your glory as You consume us with Your fire! May we be transformed from being cold or lukewarm into children of God, who are burning with Your power and manifested presence.

We put on Christ. We put on those righteous robes of glory-fire so that we are hidden in Him and He is seen, not us. We live, but it is no longer us living, but Christ living in and through us!

We proclaim as Paul did in Galatians 2:20:

> *I have been crucified with Christ and I no longer live, but Christ lives in me. The life I now live in the body, I live by faith in the Son of God, who loved me and gave Himself for me.*

Show us Your glory, and mark us with Your fire!

In Jesus' mighty name, amen!

— 4 —

THE SWELL

Surely His salvation is near those who reverence Him; our land will be filled with His glory.

Psalm 85:9 TLB

The concept of the spearhead of a greater move of God was shown to me again in another dream.

In this dream, I saw myself stepping on stones that led to the entrance of an old log cabin. When I stepped onto the threshold of the cabin's doorway, I was instantly enveloped in a brilliant light. This light was everywhere, and I entered into what I knew was a place in Heaven.

In that place, though I could not see anything but the light, I knew I was in a type of courtroom. I heard the voice of God saying, "My verdict for America has been determined. No person, no government, no legislative body can overturn My verdict!" (He was referring to the verdict, "America shall be saved!") God then said, "GO! Enforce My verdict!" Again, I couldn't see anything but the light, but I knew instinctively that when He said these words, He was pointing toward the earth.

Then I could see through the light and realized I was looking down on the United States of America. As this happened, I saw lines forming a spearhead and shaft just as I had seen in the Red River Meeting House dream. However, in this dream as I looked at those lines, I saw the spearhead was instantly lit on fire! When that happened, the entire spear began to spin counterclockwise.

The spin was slow at first, but gained speed with each spin faster and faster. As the spear was spinning, it tilted upward until it was standing vertical on the tip. The spearhead was still blazing with the fire, the spear was still spinning, and once it stood vertical, it was lifted up and then thrust with force down into the ground in the center of the United States of America.

When the spearhead went into the ground, there were swells and swells of what I thought at first were waves of water.

But this wasn't water.

The waves were people who were lit on fire! These people, moving like unending waves and waves of fire, were going out into all directions from where the spear was now standing.

And that was the end of the dream.

At the end of the Red River Meeting House dream, the spearhead formed as God made a connection between four major moves of His Spirit that took place in past times. Now He was showing us that the spear was on fire, and it was spinning counterclockwise, revealing that it is now time for the fires of all those past moves of His Spirit to culminate in a combustible force of manifested glory in our time. We have now stepped into the light, the revelation of that. Armed with the knowledge of His intentions, we are being sent by God with the authority to enforce His verdicts and to be His representatives. This move we are in now will not be a reenactment of what God has already done—it will be a combination of all the mighty works He did in those moves, and even greater. What a revelation!

How will this be possible? This fiery swell of God's unstoppable glory will be manifested in this nation and in our world through His people. God will move with the demonstration of His might through those who have surrendered their hearts and their all to Him. He will show Himself strong in and through those who are anchored on the foundation of the Word of God, and who have become living, breathing Arks of His presence (see 1 Corinthians 6:19), containers of His transforming glory, and carriers of His all-consuming fire!

One morning in prayer, I heard the Lord say to me, *"My power is twirling. It is an unstoppable spin breaking the surface to relieve the pressure of the swell of My manifested glory."* I knew He was using the word "swell" in the sense of a collection of waves that forms one long, massive, continuous wave! He continued, *"Reformation is pushing forth! The die has been cast! It cannot be stopped! The geyser is ready to be released, and what has been concealed will now be revealed! Watch it gush forth and release the pressure of the swell and reveal the fiery wave of My prevailing glory!"*

The thrusting of the fiery spear into the center of this nation was clearly revealing that awakening has begun. Holy Spirit is now releasing an unstoppable movement of a wave of glory that will spread across the nation and around the world. It is the glory of the presence of the Lord as He flows through His glorious Church. No power from hell can stop the mighty move of God that is already set into motion. This is a defining moment that has the power to change everything!

SPIRIT AND TRUTH

Recently, the Lord gave me a revelation that has enlightened me with understanding for our times. He showed me that the movement we are now in is a movement of Spirit *and* truth. It is wisdom and revelation in the knowledge of Christ that produces through us the exceeding greatness of His might—not just with words, but with power and demonstration.

There seems to be a very real and practical demonstration in the lives of true believers that is about to become light to the world as darkness has taken its toll on our nation and our world. All we have learned in the Word, by the Spirit and through our experiences with God along our journey, is about to launch us into the place of true effectiveness in our society. No more hiding behind church walls seeking emotional gratification and inspiration while all that identifies us to the world is the fact that we are church-goers.

Now is when the true Church is rising up with a revelation of who we are in Christ, marked and known by the demonstration of the reality of a life lived in Kingdom covenant. I believe the spark ignited by such a life and such living will be so powerful that it will burst out in a move of God that will revolutionize this nation, even our world.

This is what history calls *an awakening.* When we awaken to the reality of Who God really is, who we really are in Him, and to the power of all that He has made available to us, and we begin making it our priority to become all He has anointed us to be, we will be a holy, set-apart people. We will be easily recognizable in our society—not by our appearance and church attendance, but by the glory of God's presence demonstrated in our lives and living—*all for His glory!*

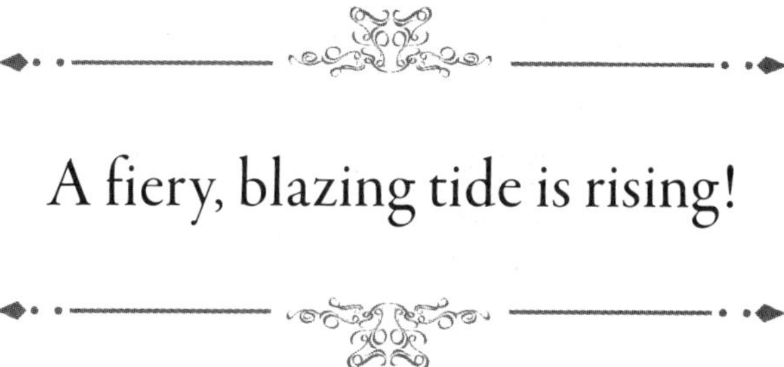

I see a tide rising! It's a fiery, blazing tide of uncompromised, bold, anointed warriors whose focus is on the Lord! Their ears hear His voice. Their feet march to the rhythm of His sound! Not everyone, even in the Church, will hear this sound and move with Him, for many are deafened by the noise of the propagated chaos and blinded by the deception operating by a spirit of fear.

But! There is a company rising—a remnant within the remnant—who are not moved by the chaos and not being driven by fear, they are being ignited by the spear of God's prophesied awakening. They are confident in Christ, and they carry the fire. God's presence shines on them and through them!

I see this wave of fiery people beginning to rise! A holy, unstoppable pushback—a swell of glory! Not against flesh and blood; that's not our fight! This is a pushing back of darkness! I can feel the rumble as the rise begins to form to release the pressure of the swell that has been waiting for this precise moment in time.

Pray with me:

Father, the fiery swell of Your unstoppable glory is beginning to manifest in this nation and in our world through Your remnant people. Awakening has begun, maybe not in the entire Church, but there is a remnant that has been awakened, and we are returning to You with an unquenchable passion that will not allow us to accept an environment that is void of Your presence. We are saturated with the oil of Your Spirit. We have been pierced and marked with the arrows of Your glory. We are ignited with the flames of awakening, and we will be unstoppable initiators of revival. We will be the wave that carries the fire of Your demonstrated glory to the earth!

You are our only focus. We surrender our all to You. Nothing else matters! Consume us, Lord! May Christ be formed in us, and may it be Christ Who lives through us! We will go for You! We will burn for You! We will shine for You, not because we want to be seen or known, but because we have been consumed by You!

Your Word is like fire shut up in our bones, and we will not hold it back. We cannot hold it back! We declare, "Release us, Lord!" Let wave after wave after wave of Your glory flow into us and through us! We will be Your voice that echoes the desires and intentions of Your heart! We will be the carriers of the flame of Yahweh!

Father, remove anything from our lives and thought processes that would cause us to be resistant to the flames of Your glory. Ignite us! May the revelation of Christ be seen as a light that shines through our lives, bringing hope to those in darkness. May that light be received, enlightening their eyes and destroying confining shackles from their minds, bodies, and spirits, freeing them to see and know You for themselves. We declare that the Body of Christ arises now with undaunted resolved to allow Holy Spirit to operate in us and through us with the power and demonstration of the exceeding greatness of Your might.

Make us Your fuel, flame of God, and release us as a wave, filled with the manifestation of Your fiery presence, covering the earth with the revelation of the glory as the waters cover the sea!

In the holy name of Jesus, amen!

— 5 —

THE ARROWS ARE DROPPING

But [the time is coming when] the earth shall be filled with the knowledge of the glory of the Lord.

Habakkuk 2:14 AMP

Just over a year after having the Red River Meeting House dream, God gave me another dream to continue that revelation.

In this dream, I was standing with someone on a deck-like structure in a very lofty place in the heavens. From this place we were looking down, *observing* the United States of America. I didn't know who the man was standing next to me, but I could feel a strong anointing about him, and his presence was causing me to have an indescribable hope for the nation!

As we were looking down, we saw what first appeared to be warplanes flying over the United States. The gentleman next to me nonchalantly said, "Oh my, I wonder what is happening in America? And what do all of these warplanes mean?" He said this, not with concern, but almost as though he wanted me to see something that wasn't obvious. He looked at me as if I should know the right answer to his questions.

I said, "Those are not warplanes. Those are eagles! I have seen them before in a dream. There are one hundred of them, and they are carrying the water from the well of revival that has been unlocked and is now gushing forth into the nation." (I was referring to the eagles I saw in the Red River Meeting House dream.)

Then I could clearly see that the eagles, just as in the Red River Meeting House dream, were carrying arrows in one talon and a rolled-up piece of paper in the other talon. They were still drenched with and releasing the water from the geyser that had burst forth on the grounds of the Red River Meeting House.

As the eagles were flying across America in all directions, suddenly they simultaneously began to dive down toward the land. It appeared as if they would crash into the ground, but they leveled off and began to drop their arrows into the land. I knew there were one hundred eagles and that each eagle carried three arrows, so there were 300 arrows released at various places throughout the land. When each arrow hit the ground, it ignited as though it had hit a gas pocket. Up from that spot came a spiraling plume of fire.

Then the man and I watched as the water the eagles were carrying and releasing—from the gushing well at the Red River Meeting House—was now being ignited by the fire from the places where the arrows had hit the ground. The water they were releasing was an extremely flammable

> substance, and it instantly caught the fire until it seemed that all of the United States was on fire.
>
> In the dream I fell to my knees and began to sob uncontrollably, as I became *very* aware of the power and presence of God!
>
> The gentleman with me began to speak under a heavy anointing, and I noticed that he had a very strong accent. He said, "You have seen correctly! This is how America will be saved! *Do not doubt it!* There is coming a sweeping move of the Spirit of God that will ignite the land with the fire of His presence and will bring a swift and undeniable awakening to an awareness of God. What seems to be one thing is about to be revealed as another thing. Some fear because of how things appear, but others *see* with holy awe and expectation! The eagles are on assignment. They carry fire power. They carry glory. At the precise moment, their arrows will be released, and they will hit their targets, and the move of God will ignite and spread very quickly!"
>
> And then he said again, "DO NOT DOUBT IT!"
>
> Still on my knees, I looked up at the man, and I then somehow knew that he was Duncan Campbell, one of the ministers from the great Hebrides revival.

And that was the end of the dream.

In this dream, we once again see the analogy of the connection of what *was* with what *is* and what is to come. Duncan Campbell represents a major move of God that took place in the Hebrides Islands, off the coast of Scotland, between 1949 and 1952. The revival fires that burned in those islands were so life-changing and transforming that multitudes of sinners were born again and forever marked by the power of God they experienced in those days.

So it is of great significance that God put this man in the dream. That great past move of God was a witness, speaking into this current move of God, in essence saying, "He who transformed *our* nation, will also come in like manner to transform *your* nation. Do not doubt it!" The transforming power of God that came in that day is still the same for us in our time. This is how America will be saved!

DROP THE ARROWS

I believe this dream is a clear indication that it's time for the dropping of the arrows that will ignite the fires of revival in the United States and in our world! Strategic pockets of revival history and prophetic purposes are being targeted by the Lord. He knows where they are, and He has planned for this moment. Ahead of time He has equipped prophets and prophetic intercessors with the piercing anointing to open the fiery wells and ignite the land with the demonstration of His power and glory as we move in obedience to the leading of Holy Spirit.

Even now, thousands of people are being called to gather in these strategic places to make a unified appeal to Heaven for the fulfilling of God's promised awakening. He is ordering our steps, directing our prayers, and provoking our decrees that will now ignite the revealing of His glory.

Two very significant aspects of releasing an arrow:

1. Arrows are piercing. They leave an undeniable mark on whatever they hit.

2. Releasing an arrow is well-timed and intentional. If an arrow hits a target, it's because it was specifically aimed at that target.

God knows where the fire pockets are. He knows the precise moment for the necessity of their revealing, and He is releasing the anointing to pierce and strike this land to create an ignition of the demonstration of His power! Watch for this to happen quickly. Pay attention to and do not disregard the movement. Stay focused, and stay in expectation. It may seem small at first, but small campfires quickly become blazing fires that bring forth eye-opening, unavoidable confrontations with the reality of our all-powerful, all-consuming God.

Do not doubt this!

Pray with me:

Almighty God, pierce us with the arrows of Your power that will forever mark us with Your transforming glory. Release the fire of Your Spirit. Saturate us with the flammable waters of the knowledge of Your well-timed wisdom and prophetic purposes so we can catch and carry the fire and release it through our obedience, prayers, and decrees to prepare the way for the ignition of the demonstration of Your glory.

We will be tuned in and convinced of Your intentions, moving with correct perception of what is happening around us so we can run with what we have received.

We declare that we will not see through the lens of our natural understanding—we see with holy awe and expectation as Holy Spirit imparts to us the wisdom and revelation of Your plan and perspective. We will operate with the supernatural precision of Your timing to release the fire power and the glory of Your presence that ignites this world and unlocks the prophetic destiny that You have purposed for lives, territories, and nations.

We resist fear! Our focus is on You! Our ears are attentive to Your leading. We will hear Your words, and we will not doubt what You say! We believe You, and we know and are convinced that what You have said, are saying, and will say shall come to pass in the right time to accomplish every purpose for which You have spoken.

In the name of Jesus we pray, amen!

— 6 —

RELEASE THE RIVER

[The Lord replied,] "Look among the nations! See! Be astonished! Wonder! For I am doing something in your days—you would not believe it if you were told."

Habakkuk 1:5 AMP

Through these previous four dreams, we get a glimpse of the magnitude of the move of the Spirit we have entered. The past moves that occurred throughout history are part of the water of revival that we are to carry. The level of the experiences the people had with God during those times was great, but it was only a measure of what was to come. Each move of God intensified and offered deeper encounters and revelation from the Lord. Each move was a "widening of the banks," allowing the river of revival anointing to run deeper and with greater force as it flowed from generation to generation.

Now it's our time to get in the river and allow it to increase with even greater measure the demonstrated glory of God and revelation of Jesus.

I believe a company of people are now feeling those waters of revival, awakening them to an awareness of the nearness of God—and we are ready. Our times with the Lord in persistent intercession and humble obedience has left us saturated with the oil of His Spirit, making us susceptible to receive His flame. Our hearts are filled with anticipation of

His clarion signal to rise and carry the water and fire of His transforming glory. It's time, and we are rightly postured to receive and carry out the instructions, assignments, and purposes He has drawn up for us in our time.

Our goal is not to gain the attention and applause of people. Our focus is on Christ, and our desire is that His Kingdom comes and His will is done on earth as it is in Heaven (see Matthew 6:9-10). We are inspired by what He has done, but we won't settle in the confining idea that He is finished!

We burn with the expectation that what He has done, He will do that again and even greater. We are taking our place on the timeline of history. We are those Rapid Response Teams who will run with the purposes of our righteous King. We enter into this move, wholly devoted to Him. "Bend us and send us" is the cry of our hearts.

In response the Lord replies, *"Through you I will now begin to reveal My manifested glory. As you arise, I will arise, and every enemy will scatter! Watch and see and be amazed by what I will do in days ahead through My awakened Body."*

SECTION TWO

— 7 —

FIND THE ANCIENT PATH

And the Lord shall guide thee continually, and satisfy thy soul in drought, and make fat thy bones: and thou shalt be like a watered garden, and like a spring of water, whose waters fail not. And they that shall be of thee shall build the old waste places: thou shalt raise up the foundations of many generations; and thou shalt be called, The repairer of the breach, The restorer of paths to dwell in.

Isaiah 58:11-12 KJV

A few years ago, I had a vision.

In this vision I saw myself and three friends walking down a path. It wasn't a well-beaten path; it was formed just enough that we could see where to go.

Ahead of us, we saw a pile of debris. There were dead trees, branches, and leaves blocking the path. Determined to follow this path, the four of us walked up to the pile and began the task of removing the debris. Once the debris was removed, we suddenly could see a very well-formed path,

> and we realized we were seeing this path through a large keyhole. The keyhole seemed to be about five or six feet tall. Then all of a sudden, we had an old, large skeleton key in our possession. So we put that key into the keyhole, and it fit!
>
> The four of us then worked together to turn the key and open the door, and there before us was that very well-formed path. It was an old path, yet it seemed new to us. We could sense the glory of God filling the atmosphere where we were, and we could even see the glory on the path.
>
> As we stood there in awe of what we were witnessing, all of a sudden across the path in front of us these words appeared: "The Ancient Path." Then we took the first steps down this ancient path. Each step seemed to cause more and more of the path to be revealed.

That ended the vision.

I was then immediately led to the following Scripture:

> *This is what the Lord says: "Stand at the crossroads and look; ask for the ancient paths, ask where the good way is, and walk in it, and you will find rest for your souls..."* (Jeremiah 6:16 NIV).

In the previous section of this book, I shared with you some of the dreams God has given to me about awakening and revival. In those dreams, and even in the Scriptures, the Lord often used the concept of rivers and fire to illustrate and define the movement of the Spirit. As stated earlier, God spoke to the priests in the temple about the fire on the altar, instructing them that it must never go out (see Leviticus 6:13).

Then in Leviticus 9:24 we read that the *"Fire came out from the presence of the Lord...."* The fire originated in God. He is the all-consuming Fire (Hebrews 12:29).

In Ezekiel 47, we see the illustration of the river that flowed, representing the stages of the movement of the Spirit of God—ankle deep, knee deep, waist deep, and then waters to swim in. This healing river that brought life to everything it touched, was flowing out of the temple of God. Revelation 22:1 tells us that this river originated from the throne of God and of the Lamb, Jesus Christ.

In the second chapter of Acts, we read how the Church was birthed as those 120 men and women gathered in the upper room and encountered the God of fire. The fire of God's glory and Spirit did not just come among them, it came *into* them, empowering them to be effective witnesses for Christ in the world. The fire that started in God—the Fire that *is* God—was now dwelling inside the Church.

In John 7:38-39 (NIV), Jesus was speaking of those who would believe in Him. He said of these people that *"rivers of living water will flow from within them."* He was speaking of Holy Spirit Who dwells in us as born-again believers, and flows out through us with power to reveal Christ to the world around us.

RETURN TO GOD

My point in drawing our attention to these passages is to help us understand that the fire comes out of God. The river flows from Him. *He* is the origination point. It starts in Him and then flows and burns in us to reveal Him to the world. This is and has always been His plan, to have a people through whom He can manifest His love, power, and glory. So when He instructs us in Jeremiah 6:16 (NIV) to *"ask for the ancient paths,"* He is not speaking of denominational doctrine or human traditions—He is speaking of Himself. He is speaking of His original plans and intentions.

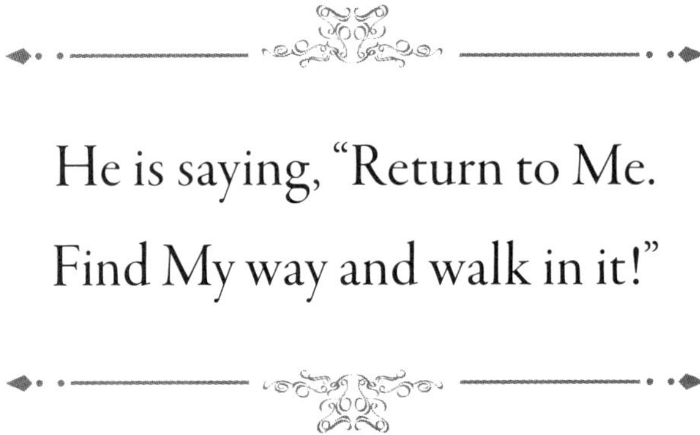

He is saying, "Return to Me. Find My way and walk in it!"

We don't create a way that seems right to us and just jump in and do our own thing and call it revival. The way is already there. Although it has been covered over by the debris of human ways and ideology, thus fading the *true* path, there are those rising up and realizing there is an ancient path, and we are going to look for it and ask for it. Jesus is the Way, and we will ask Him to lead us.

God has given us the key—faith in Him. We must turn our focus off ourselves and onto God. As we return to Him, He will return to us, and the Way will be opened to us, and we can walk the path that reveals the glory. We can carry the fire of God, and release the waters of the river of life that bring life, healing, and restoration (see Revelation 22:1-2). This is another aspect of awakening.

Just as with those priests in the temple, so it is with us, we are commanded to keep fervent the fire God has started. To walk the ancient path is to surrender our desires for His desires. It is to be completely His. It is to be consumed by His glory and attentive and uncompromisingly obedient to His leading. So at this moment, we must stand at the crossroads and ask for the ancient path that leads us to Him.

Show us *Your* ways, Lord, and lead us according to Your original plans and purposes. Whatever the cost, we must never let the fire go out, and we must never allow the flow of the river to wane.

In Isaiah 58, the Lord reveals that if we choose to walk according to His plan, follow His instructions, and do what He has called us to do, God:

> *will continually guide you, and satisfy your soul in scorched and dry places, and give strength to your bones; and you will be like a watered garden, and like* ***a spring of water whose waters do not fail.*** *And* ***your people will rebuild the ancient ruins;*** *you will raise up and restore the age-old foundations [of buildings that have been laid waste]; you will be called Repairer of the Breach, Restorer of Streets with Dwellings* (Isaiah 58:11-12 AMP).

What God has started is still available to us today. Regardless of how things may appear around us, we must stay focused on Jesus. We must never allow the "debris" of life to stop us from pursuing Him and the plans and intentions He has for us in our time. Those who went before us followed the path for their time, and they left us an example. Now it's our time to do our part, and leave an example for those who will come after us. They must know about the fire and the river, not just because we spoke of them, but because we allowed *the fire to burn in us*, and because we allowed *the river to flow through us*.

We must remember, honor, and raise up the ancient foundations of God's intentions. We must build our part for our time so those who come after us can build their part for their time. And what we must do cannot be done by our own might or power. The might and power come from God, and He has put that might and power in us by the indwelling of the Holy Spirit. What He started in us, He is faithful to complete in us. His plan is still moving forward. The fire is still burning, the river is still flowing, and the path is still there for us to find and follow.

The Lord spoke the following word to me a couple of years ago. Hear His heart and yield to the launching.

> *The time has come when I will begin releasing* ***through*** *My people what I have been doing* ***in*** *My people. You will now rise to a whole new level of power, demonstration, and operation of My Person and purposes.*
>
> *I Am pulling you out of a narrow place and pressing you into a large place...a place of seeing...a place of vision...a place of BE-ing. It's like waking up to a new day and realizing the old is gone, the new has come. This is your defining moment. This is your place of launching. Your orders are: "Forward!"*
>
> *I Am now separating you unto Myself. I Am calling you into deeper encounter with Me; and from My presence, you will be launched. My presence is your Command Center. It's the place of hearing, healing, knowing, seeing, receiving, and from there you will be released to release My purposes and desires.*
>
> *I Am ready to reveal this part of My plan that has long been inside Me, but now it's time. It's time. And what has been hidden will now be revealed, no longer concealed inside My heart. Now, I bring*

it forth. And those who draw near to Me will see, hear, know, and be equipped to carry and release their part as I accomplish this part of My plan on earth.

This time I have chosen as a time of launching. Now you will spring forth! I Am thrusting you forward, and you will move with clarity and unobstructed vision as you yield yourself to Me and make My presence your priority. What I do in this moment through those who draw near to Me will not and cannot be done by your own efforts. It's been Mine all along, and you will accomplish the things I send you out for. Nothing will be left undone! As long as you draw near to Me, hear from Me, look to Me, and obey Me, I will do through you what you never thought to dream.

This is the point of no return. The page has turned, and my plan for "Forward" is being set into motion. Don't look back and don't hold back. Yield yourself to Me, and I will stretch forth My hand through you to make Myself known!

The dreams in the following chapters reveal more insight into the revelation of our need to return to the Lord, to know and embrace His original intentions, and to cooperate with Holy Spirit as He works through us to make Christ known to the world around us.

— 8 —

THE RESTORATION

Who is left among you that saw this house in her first glory? and how do ye see it now? is it not in your eyes in comparison of it as nothing?

Haggai 2:3 KJV

I dreamed that:

I was standing on the lawn of a very large stately house that had been built to last! Inside, I knew the house was fully furnished and beautifully decorated.

In the dream, I knew that I had seen this house previously, and I could remember every detail about it. But as I stood on the lawn, it didn't look anything like I had remembered. Someone had placed stucco all over the outside, changing the entire look of the house. I remember thinking, *This isn't right! It's so ugly compared to its former glory!*

However, even though it appeared to have been completely changed, I somehow knew the original house was still fully intact. I knew the inside had not been changed. I also knew the original look of the house, underneath the stucco, was still exactly the same as the builder had built it. Those who had attempted to change the house did not have the authority or the ability to fully remake or remodel it, so they just put the stucco on the outside to make it appear as though the house had been totally redone.

All of a sudden, a huge geyser erupted on the front lawn. This eruption caused a massive shaking. The water from the geyser shot very high up into the sky, and the water rained down over the entire scene.

The shaking caused the stucco on the house to crack and begin to crumble. The water from the geyser then dissolved all the stucco, bringing the house back to its original state. I even saw a driveway form, and the landscaping was totally restored to its original appearance. The water had restored everything!

And that was the end of the dream.

We are being called back to the place of truly knowing God, Jesus, and Holy Spirit. I hear the Lord saying to His Church, *"I'm still here."* We've made church to be a lot of stuff that God never intended for it to be. We have plastered it with our ideas and created an atmosphere that caters to our emotions and needs, leaving no space for God to come in His power and demonstrated glory.

The Church that was birthed in the book of Acts was a Body of believers who were filled with the fire and power of Holy Spirit, and that infilling was evidenced by the operation of the Spirit in and through their everyday lives. By Holy Spirit, God equipped them with gifts and fruit that caused the world to look at them and see Christ. They devoted their lives to Christ and His cause; through them the light of the Gospel shined, and the power of God was demonstrated, enabling them to turn the world upside down for the sake of the Kingdom of God (see Acts 17:6 NKJV).

That's the way God made the Church—a living, powerful representation of Christ, not a weak, powerless entity that depends on entertainment and charismatic preachers to pep up a crowd on Sundays. As one preacher said, "God made the Church the way He wanted it, and now He wants the Church to be the way He made it."

Human traditions and platforms are about to be dissolved. The ugly façade of powerless, religious routine is about to be met with the blast of the manifested power of Holy Spirit that will bring us back to God as Father, Jesus as Savior, Healer, Deliverer, Redeemer, and Holy Spirit as Truth-Revealer and Guide. The Spirit of wisdom and revelation in the knowledge of Christ is going to sweep the Church to enlighten the eyes of our understanding. We can know the hope of His calling, the riches of the glory of His inheritance in us, and the world will see and know beyond any shadow of doubt the exceeding greatness of His power as He demonstrates through His people, the working of His mighty power!

And just as the driveway formed in my dream, so the Way will be made for others to see and know God as Father, Jesus as Savior, Healer, Deliverer, Redeemer, and Holy Spirit as Truth-Revealer and Guide.

Let's pray:

Father, we know You are beckoning us back to Yourself. The answer to the situations in our world is not another church program or rehearsed message that has lost its savor. What we need is a revelation of Jesus. What we need is a reconnection to You as Father! What we need is to be baptized afresh and anew in the Holy Spirit and fire! So we declare that the wells of revival are bursting forth and breaking off the façade!

You, Jesus, in Your beauty and glory, are coming back into view. You are changing our hearts and our minds, bringing us back to the place of vicious hunger for more and more of You! We long to step back into Your fullness and experience the real of Your power and goodness.

Father, we know that in You nothing has changed. Your gifts are still there. Your goodness is still there. You are still all-powerful, good, and wise. We know that Your original plans are still intact, and You will have Your way and receive all glory and honor.

We run back to You and step into Your presence. We make Your heart our home, and we will work from "home" to reveal the reality of You everywhere we go, making a way for everyone we meet to come in and know You for themselves.

In Jesus' name, amen!

— 9 —

THE MOST VALUABLE TREASURE

The Kingdom of Heaven is like a [very precious] treasure hidden in a field, which a man found and hid again; then in his joy he goes and sells all he has and buys that field [securing the treasure for himself]

Matthew 13:44 AMP

nother dream:

I dreamed I was in the library on the campus of the university of a major Pentecostal denomination. I knew that every part of this denomination was being prepared to be sold, including the university. Two friends of mine, whom I have not seen in many years, had been assigned to clean up the library. A very wealthy family was going to buy the denomination, and were scheduled to come and look at some of the properties the next day.

In the library, I could see that the entire front wall was a window with a door to the left side. Going out the door, there were steps leading to a sidewalk and a street. My vehicle was parked on that street. The library window had been painted with so much graffiti that I couldn't even tell it was actually a glass window.

In the dream, I had just entered the library and was walking toward one of my friends, who was there cleaning, and I saw her throw a piece of paper onto a table. The table sat in front of the graffiti-covered window, and it was almost as long as the window. The tabletop had sides around the top, about five inches deep, which was full of honey! It was so beautiful, golden, rich, and pure! I had never seen anything like it, and I instantly knew it was extremely valuable. I noticed there were a few books that had already been thrown into the honey, along with the piece of paper my friend had tossed into it. I said to her, "What are you doing?"

She said, "What do you mean what am I doing? We're just going to throw a bunch of stuff on there and take it all out at one time! Some OLD BEES got in here and made all this honey, and we're just going to get rid of it."

I was just shocked that she didn't even realize the value of the honey, and I said, "Oh, no! You can't get rid of that! THAT'S THE MOST VALUABLE THING IN HERE!"

I then started taking the books out, and scraping off every bit of the honey that I could from the books as I removed them, and also from the piece of paper my friend had thrown into it.

As I was doing that, my other friend was about to leave, and I asked her to buy and bring back for me as many plastic containers as she could find. I told her that I would repay her when she returned. Then I said, "If you'll let me, I will harvest this honey and take it with me. You can't just trash it! It's very valuable!"

She said, "Well, you can have it. Nobody here wants to fool with it, anyway. It's too messy!"

I said, "Yeah, but it doesn't matter that it's messy. It's valuable, and we can't just throw it away."

A young man and a few other people were there helping to clean up the library, and they had been curiously watching me and listening to my voiced concerns about the honey. They were in shock that I was actually determined to save it.

Then my friend returned with many super-large containers for me. I had somehow gotten a few containers before she arrived, and had already started harvesting the honey. I tried to get the others to help me, but they said, "No! We don't want to get that all over us. It's too messy!"

I had found a knife and was using it to cut the honeycomb. I was trying to cut it into manageable squares so I could get it all into the containers. I finally talked my friend into helping me to, at least, cut the honeycomb. I filled up the containers with honey. I was digging in! I tried not to get a lot on me because I didn't want to waste any of it. I was determined to get all that I possibly could, no matter what.

After I got the most of it out, I then tilted the table up, and with my hands I carefully scraped every last bit of the honey that I possibly could into the containers. Again, I didn't want to waste any of it!

I worked on this all through the night. Everyone left, except the young man who had been there helping clean the library. In the early morning hours, after I harvested all the honey that I could, the young man helped me carry the containers out to my vehicle. There was a huge amount of honey, which was very heavy! We loaded my vehicle and a large U-Haul trailer, which I was towing, with all of the honey-filled containers.

I went back into the library and realized I had left the table tilted up on its end. So I lowered it back to the floor. I didn't lower it with a thud. I just placed it back on the floor—but when I did, the sound went through that graffiti-covered glass window, and all of a sudden, the window completely shattered into tiny pieces. Neither I nor the young man seemed shocked by this, at all! We just swept up the glass pieces. After we swept up all the pieces, a brand-new window instantly formed in that opening!

By this time, it was early morning and my friends and the other workers had returned to finish cleaning the library. It was a mess. I asked my friends, "How did it get like this? This place is a mess! I can't believe people just allowed it to get in this condition!"

I then noticed how the workers were moving very slowly, just walking around, looking at one book at a time, picking up each one off the floor, and reading through them. Knowing that the buyers were coming that day, I said to them, "Just leave that stuff alone! That's not important now! You don't have time to look at every book. You should have *done* that already! You should have already read them, and you should know what's in them. You will just have to find what is the most important things, and throw everything else away. You don't have time now to try to look through everything."

I then called a friend, who is an organizer, and asked her to come and help. When she arrived, I told the workers, "Listen to her. She will help you know what to do. You're going to have to gather up only what's necessary and throw everything else away. You just have to KNOW what matters!" So, as my friend instructed us, we all worked on getting everything picked up.

Finally, the library was pretty much cleaned. I was standing by the door getting ready to leave, when a group of businessmen, dressed in very expensive suits, walked in. There were about ten of them. Nine were lawyers who represented the family who was prepared to purchase the denomination. The other man with them was actually a member of the family who was buying the denomination. As they walked in, this man immediately walked over to the table where the honey had been, and he looked rather disappointed that the honey was no longer there.

He ran his finger through the sticky residue left on the table, then licked it off his finger.

"Where's the honey?"

One of my long-ago friends who had been in charge of cleaning the library said, "Oh, don't worry about that. We got rid of all of *that* messy stuff!"

He said, "That's too bad! I would have bought this whole place just to have that honey!"

I knew the honey was what they had wanted all along, and they had talked the denomination into selling out just so they could have it.

He looked over at me and he said, "Whoever has that honey has a rare treasure, and they saved it just in time! They should do right by it, because that honey is real, it's rare, and it's VERY valuable. You can hardly find it anymore!"

All the while he was looking right at me. I still had some of the honey on me where I had harvested it into the containers, so I was sure he knew I had it!

He then said, "There are people who would give everything they own just to have that honey!"

I walked out the door and got in my vehicle. Not even looking back, I pulled away with all of that honey. As I drove away, I was sobbing. I was weeping because the people in the library and in the denomination didn't realize the value of the honey. I was also weeping because I was so grateful that I had been able to "save" it from those who were going to misuse it.

And that was the end of the dream.

Today, there is almost an embarrassment that shrouds many who were raised with a Pentecostal background. In an attempt to separate themselves from this rich heritage, some choose to hide and discredit what the "old bees" left behind to pursue social acceptance that could bring church growth that did not require "messy" devotion. But the truth is that Church without the "honey" is equivalent to form without power.

PRESERVE THE HONEY

Having grown up in Pentecostalism, I do understand that everything that was done in past generations was not an accurate picture of what God intended the Church to be, nor was it all part of the treasure intended by God to be passed down to future generations. Legalism and traditionalism began to invade the Church, causing many to become servants to the system instead of pursuant lovers of God. Fear of people gripped the hearts of many, as leaders moved in pride and church politics that brought division, control, prayerlessness, and lifeless form.

The window of revelation was painted over by human doctrines, hiding the most valuable treasure we possess—the manifested glory of God. Even today, many within the Church still operate under the influence of confining religious spirits seeking to control and manipulate the move of God.

Nevertheless, there *were* those who walked in true devotion to and dependency on God, which enabled them to encounter Him in His transforming glory. They walked in an honor and reverence to God, and their worship to Him was pure and sincere. Though simple and maybe a little distasteful now, that heartfelt worship captured the attention of Heaven, not only giving them access to God, but it gave God access to them because He comes where He is truly acknowledged. The fire of God was not only talked about among those devoted saints, it was experienced—and their experience with God is now a witness declaring His mighty acts to our generation (see Psalm 145:4).

The pride that now tries to convince the Church that we're more sophisticated and we don't need that "old stuff" has invaded the hearts of many, and compromise has caused us to trade power and glory for cultural relevance and acceptance. To dishonor and forsake what was truly of God in the past generations is to destroy the very foundation on which we are meant to build.

Without the foundation of Christ as the Chief Cornerstone, what we have built has become vulnerable and susceptible to the winds of change that are now blowing into our culture, causing many of our churches to be labeled as "nonessential."

Sadly, we now have a generation that doesn't really know God in the fullness of His power. They may know *of* Him, but the demonstration of His life-changing glory is a foreign concept to them. The nonappealing, lifeless form that has been settled for in the past decades has now left many without an ability to stand against the raging tide of hell's attempt to overthrow and dismantle the Church.

Unwilling to reform and realign with God's original plans and intentions, many have chosen to "sell out" to compromise. The generations before us may not have done everything right, but they also did not do everything wrong! They walked in the light they had, and they experienced God on levels that many of our churches are unfamiliar with today. The power of God that was seen and experienced among them was undeniable, and countless stories of healings, transformed lives, deliverances, transformed cities, towns, and communities was the undeniable fruit that was produced by those Pentecostal roots. This is the true treasure that has been passed down to us as an inheritance and meant to be experienced in our times!

AWAKENED WARRIORS

Now, there is a company of awakened warriors who are remembering the "honey," the most valuable treasure. What we have had in the past few decades has paled in comparison to what was experienced in previous generations, and many are now being shaken by the realization that something is missing in our modern church experience. God is shattering the painted windows that have veiled the true power available to all who will receive what He has given. He is creating a window of opportunity revealing the pure—and with the revealing comes the invitation to taste and receive what has been available all along.

In the dream, I knew the value of the honey and that it must be saved. That is not to say that I believe I am the only one who understands the value of this treasure. While some may choose to stay the course of compromise, there are many others who have had a glimpse and taste of what is available. They are more than willing to roll up their sleeves and recapture the treasure of Pentecostal fire that is our rightful inheritance. We refuse to sell out to those who have no appreciation for this costly treasure. We choose to be the containers that receive and carry the "honey" of God's rich and pure glory!

Time has accelerated. We have now moved into a major, defining moment with God. We are being weighed in the balance. The truth is, the scales could tip in either direction, but the weightiness of His presence, carried and allowed to be demonstrated by those who are unwilling to settle for a powerless form, will now tip the scales in the direction of revival awakening that will save America and the nations of the world!

Yahweh is calling His Church to rise and be the true Body of Christ, functioning in the power and likeness of our Savior. We do not have time to hesitate. We must go after the pure! We must now gather up our experiences, realign with what is truly of God, and rise as the uncompromised Body of Christ demonstrating the fullness of God to the world around us. We *must* be that generation that saves the honey so we may experience this treasure of glory and pass the faith along to those who will come after us.

Please pray with me:

Father, forgive us for compromise. Restore to us the revelation of our inheritance. Awaken in us a passionate desire to pursue You and all that You have made available to us by Your Spirit. Resurrect in us a recognition of and cooperation with Holy Spirit and His powerful work in and through our lives.

You have called Your Church to attention, and we will respond to that call. We refuse to settle! We refuse to compromise! We refuse to hide the flame of Pentecostal fire and power! We gladly receive the fullness of all that You desire to pour into and out through our lives. We pray for those who have settled, but we refuse to allow the compromise of others to stop our pursuit of the operation of the fullness of the valuable treasure of Your pure manifested glory working in and among us. May our lives be a window revealing Christ. May others look at our lives and see Him, Christ in us the hope of glory being revealed through us!

Father, we avail ourselves to You. Where You lead us, we will follow. What You desire to say to us, we will listen to and hear. Whatever You desire to do in us and through us, we will obey. We don't mind the mess! More of You, less of us. We are Your vessels, and we cry, "Fill us up with Your glory!" Amen!

— 10 —

TRAILBLAZERS

I once had a dream in which God revealed the necessity for the Church to go beyond where we have been; and as forerunners, we were to deal with whatever seeks to block our forward progress to advance and clear a path for others to follow.

I dreamed I was with a group of people at the base of a very large, tall mountain. There was an old logging road in front of us, leading toward the top of the mountain. This road had not been used in a *very* long time. It was overgrown, but it could be seen and used. We knew that the old road only went so far up the mountain, but our plan was to follow that old path as best we could and then continue on where it left off. We knew we had to get to the top of that mountain.

Some people there were telling us that it was not wise for us to use that old road. "You shouldn't be doing that! This road only goes so far, and no one has ever gone beyond the point where it ends."

Dutch Sheets—who to me represents the apostolic and prophetic prayer movement in America—then spoke up and said, "It's time to build the House of God! We *must* go to the top of this mountain!" In our entire group there was a determination to make the journey—regardless the cost—to get to where we needed to be and complete the task we had been assigned.

Each person in our group got into vehicles there for our use. I had never seen anything like these vehicles. They looked like an odd shaped truck but with no wheels; instead there were tracks like on a tank or bulldozer. They were green and looked like some type of military vehicle.

Each of us had one of these vehicles. Each was exactly as I described, except the one in the front of the line had a dozer blade on the front of it. We all followed *that* truck up the old road.

We went a long way and then came to the end of the road. Lying across the end of the old road was a *huge* snake. It was so large that our vehicles could not cross over it. It was massive—about four feet thick—and it was enormous in length. It was so real in the dream that it was as if I could hear and feel it breathing. It wasn't aggressive, and it didn't try to attack us; nevertheless, it was blocking our way up the mountain.

We all got out of our vehicles and began praying in tongues. The lady, who had been at the base of the mountain telling us that we shouldn't go up this road, had followed us, and she said, "I told you that you can't go here! You can't go past this point. No one has gone past this point before." Then she made a very odd statement, "It's the year of the snake!"

Dutch then rose up with a righteous indignation and a confident boldness and declared emphatically, "IT IS *NOT* THE YEAR OF THE SNAKE! THIS IS THE ERA

OF THE KING, AND OUR KING IS SEATED AND HIGHLY EXALTED!"

We all got back into our vehicles, and my friend and fellow intercessor, Dr. Don Lynch, got out of his vehicle and walked up to where the old road ended. There was a very large sword that had been left there. Its tip was stuck into the ground, and it was positioned as though left specifically for us to find and use.

The sword was almost as tall as Don. It was heavy, but he put his hands on the handle, lifted the sword, and wielded it as though it were made just for him! There was a strong anointing on him as he did this. He walked the length of the snake until he came to its head, and with that sword he cut off the snake's head! The snake didn't writhe; it didn't even move. It just deflated like a tire losing air! We could hear as the air went out of it. It went completely flat, leaving nothing but the skin.

Dr. Don got into his vehicle, and we continued up the mountain. We just rolled over what was left of the snake. The truck in front, the one with the dozer blade, was clearing a path. The ride was very rough because this truck was carving the way, but as each of our trucks followed, we were defining the road more and more.

When we reached the top of the mountain, the ground was very level. There was a building there that looked just like the building I saw in the House of God dream you read about in Chapter 1 in this book. We got out of our vehicles, and someone in our group shouted, "It's time to build the House of God!"

> Dutch then instructed us, "Do not get enthralled with the movement...build the House of God!"
>
> Someone pointed to one of the trucks and asked, "What *are* these things? I've never seen anything like them."
>
> Someone else answered, "They are called Trailblazers, and we are the forerunners to drive them. It was our time to pick up where the old road ended and extend the path. We are called to go beyond so we can build our part on the House of God for our time."

And that's all I remember about the dream.

As already mentioned in this book, I have tremendous honor and gratitude for the people who took their place to do their part in the plan of God for their times. Years ago, the Lord gave me a clear revelation and understanding that if those who lived before us had not done what they did, we would not have what we have, nor would we be able to do what we can do now.

That is true concerning natural things as well as spiritual. Their dedication to God and determination to walk with Him in obedience to His leading cleared a path for us to follow. They completed their task, and they left for us an example so that we are equipped with understanding and revelation that enables us to know God, hear Him, trust Him, and follow Him to complete the assignments and purposes He has for our lives in our time.

In 2 Timothy 1:5 (NLT), Paul makes a statement to Timothy that shows us the example of passing the faith along, and how that faith grows with each generation:

> I remember your genuine faith, for you share the faith that first filled your grandmother Lois and your mother, Eunice. And I know that same faith continues strong in you.

He then instructed Timothy to continue that faith and fan into flames the gifts in him. Because of what others did in their time, Timothy recognized his purpose and could run on with what he had been given to fulfill what God called and equipped him to do in his generation.

This dream instructs us not to stop with what others did before us. Their trail went as far as God wanted it to go, but that was not a stopping point for us; that was a marking point telling us, "Start here, and *keep going*!" Job said, *"The righteous keep moving forward, and those with clean hands become stronger and stronger"* (Job 17:9 NLT). In John 4:38, Jesus says we have entered into the labors of others. It's the same concept as what was depicted in this dream.

FORGE AHEAD

We started out following the trail that had been blazed by others, who had gone before. We made progress because others did their part and left us a road to follow. Now, as the book of Hebrews reveals, those who went before us are seated as the great cloud of witnesses. I believe their good works and undaunted faith in God now echo encouragement that compels us to continue and *"run with endurance the race that is set before us"* (Hebrews 12:1 NKJV).

Some Christians try to make us believe that we can't advance any farther down the path. They try to convince us that what others did before us was all that needed to be done and that the end of the path is as far as we can go with God. But nothing could be further from the truth. We are never meant to veer off the original path, but we *are* meant to continue and advance the path. There is work yet to be done, and this is our time to advance and build.

Paul explains in Ephesians 2 that God is building for Himself a dwelling place, and He is using every generation in what He is building.

> *God is building a home. He's using us all—irrespective of how we got here—in what He is building. He used the apostles and prophets for the foundation. Now He's using you, fitting you in brick by brick, stone by stone, with Christ Jesus as the cornerstone that holds all the parts together. We see it taking shape day after day—a holy temple built by God, all of us built into it, a temple in which God is quite at home* (Ephesians 2:20-22 MSG).

Paul tells us that we are the temple of God and that the Spirit of God dwells in us (see 1 Corinthians 3:16). The Body of Christ is being built up to be a habitation for God. As each part does its work, through us, He will reveal His power and might.

The enemy would love to block our path, deter us, contain us, and keep us from advancing, but we must boldly and confidently wield the sword of the Lord, the Word of God, to cut off the head of the enemy. We *must* keep moving forward. This is not the time for fear and weariness, this is the era of the King, and our King is seated and highly exalted. We do not focus on what the devil is doing. We are focused on our righteous King who is seated in authority and power, and we believe and declare His Words.

We tune out the noise of the naysayers and hear and follow the leading of our Guide. We will not retreat. We will not back up. We will not stop until He says we are done. We will break through and advance, and we will experience the glory of God as He comes to move among us. Our focus will not be on "the move" and the manifestations of God that accompany the move. Our focus will remain on the God of the move, for it is unto Him we are separated, and it is for Him alone that we live!

It's all about God's plan!

Holy Spirit is our Guide, and He is going before us to the open the way that reveals the path forward. And the path forward is never just about us; it's all about God's plan. It's about the future He's leading us and others into. Our personal obedience to God's leading is a vital part of our journey. We are a body—people connected to people. Countless others are dependent on our obedience to God because they can't get into *their* place until we get into *our* place!

We are not only living this life for ourselves. We are leaving a trail for others to follow. We are forerunners, and we must do our part to prepare the way and make a highway to blaze a trail. Why are we to do this? So *"The glory of the Lord shall be revealed"* (Isaiah 40:5 NKJV) in our times and for those who will follow the path we leave behind.

Let's pray and declare:

Father, we hear You calling us to go beyond the familiar routine. We feel the pull of Holy Spirit as He guides us into uncharted territory to reach the heights of Your intended purposes for our generation. It's time, and we choose to follow His lead. We wield the sword of the Word of God that destroys every attempt of the enemy to stop our advancement. We choose to listen to You, and to silence all other voices—including our own—that seek to convince us that what has been is all there is. We will not settle. We stay the course. We trust You to show us the way.

We honor the generations who took their place in Your plan for their time and blazed a trail for us. Throughout our history, many prayers have been prayed that have resulted in many mighty moves of God that have been instrumental in keeping the Church and this nation on track with Your intended purposes. We continue to build on the foundation that was laid.

We do not try to re-do what has already been done. Rather, we take hold of what has been passed to us and enter into the labors of those who have gone before us. We join our prayers with their prayers to make a synergistic appeal to Heaven for Your purpose of the ages to be done in our time and in our land!

Armed with Your Word, we advance with the anointing to "go beyond" and be a people in whom You can dwell and through whom Christ can be made known.

Lead us, Lord, and we will follow!

Amen!

— 11 —

AWAKENING HAS BEGUN

You may be wondering, *What do these dreams have to do with revival and awakening?* Truth is, they have everything to do with revival and awakening. God is the Treasure, and as we recognize the value of His presence and become willing to pursue Him at any cost, awakening happens. As the Ekklesia—the praying Church, God's governing Body—works in obedience to God and in cooperation with Holy Spirit, movement begins to happen. Examine these truths:

- The more we draw near to Him, the more He will draw near to us.
- The closer we are to God, the more we will hear and know His will.
- The more we hear and are convinced of His will, the more obedient we are to Him.
- The more obedient we are to His leading, the more we will experience the manifestation of His goodness and power.

His involvement in our lives then becomes a witness that shouts the reality of Jesus and the goodness of God to people around us and to those who come after us, provoking an awakening to an awareness of God that will burn in our time and continue for generations to come!

God's greatest desire for the Body of Christ is that we know Him by experience. God says in Jeremiah:

> *Don't let the wise brag of their wisdom. Don't let heroes brag of their exploits. Don't let the rich brag of their riches. If you brag, brag of this and this only: That you understand and know Me. I'm God, and I act in loyal love. I do what's right and set things right and fair, and delight in those who do the same things. These are My trademarks...* (Jeremiah 9:24 MSG).

Our submission to God gives Him access to work in our lives; and while we delight in the fruit of His manifested presence, that fruit must remain. Our lives must be lived as a testimony blazing a trail for others to follow. God's intentions were never that the Church operates in a lifeless form of Christianity. His desire is for us to be like Christ, clothed in His righteousness and functioning in His victorious power.

We are His witnesses. We know Him, and we are called to make Him known. We have experienced Him, and now He says we are to go forth bearing the unmistakable signs of His trademarks in and through our lives, carrying the reality of Jesus into all our spheres of influence. That is the provocation of awakening and revival!

One morning, during a time of prayer, I heard the Lord say, *"There is a Joseph company arising. They are a prepared people who are ready to be released into a prepared moment as I unveil through them another part of My unstoppable plan!"*

I once dreamed that I was with many intercessors who were gathered in a field. We were all on horses. It was like a scene in a movie as a leader rallies his troops. Dutch Sheets was there, praying over the team. Then my friend Dr. Don Lynch (who to me represents a true apostolic father), rode out in front of us and began a victory chant, shouting the word "VICTORY!" several times. He began to weep, and he said, "Our victory is secured!" He then held up a silver coin and said, "We are not fighting *for* victory, we are fighting *with* victory!"

Then he gave each of us one of the same coins. I looked at it and saw a cross embossed on one side and the Liberty Bell and a pair of combat boots embossed on the other side. Both sides had the word VICTORY written across the top of it.

Dr. Don returned to the group, and Dutch held up the coin and said, "It's time to change the way we've been thinking! We are now fighting *with* victory! Victory belongs to Jesus!" He then looked off into the distance, and pointing toward the east he said, "It's time!" I remember the sky looked dark, but there were visible shafts of sunlight breaking through, dappling the field in the direction he was pointing. So we all turned our horses and rode in that direction in a slow trot at first, and then at full gallop!

That's all I remember of the dream.

The coin we were each given in the dream reveals that Jesus' finished work on the Cross has secured our victory. Our liberty is in Him. Victory belongs to Jesus, and we are in Christ, and by Him we always triumph. We are not striving to gain victory—in Christ, we have already been given access to the victory He accomplished on the Cross. We must set our minds to this truth!

Jesus rose from the grave, and He ascended to Heaven where He is seated at the right hand of Father, God (see Hebrews 8:1). Paul, writing to the Church at Ephesus, said that through Christ, grace has been extended to us, by which we are saved. As born-again heirs with God, He has seated us with Christ in the Heavenly places (see Ephesians 2:4-6). This is a revelation of the authority that we have in Christ Jesus.

As our minds and spirits are set with this revelation, we successfully resist the work of *"all principality and power and might and dominion, and every name that is named, not only in this age but also in that which is to come"* (Ephesians 1:21 NKJV), and we are empowered to accomplish every purpose for which we have been sent, looking to Jesus, the Victor—Jesus, the Author and Finisher of our faith (see Hebrews 12:2).

Let's agree together:

Father, we look around and can clearly see that we have stepped into the beginning of another great awakening. It is time! At the onset of this major moment, we hear You calling us back to You. Forgive us, Lord, for following You from afar. Lead us back to that ancient path that not only connects us to what You have done, but points us in the direction of what You desire to do in and through us now. We feel and will readily respond to Holy Spirit's drawing, as He leads us back to Your presence.

There is a remnant within the Church who isn't satisfied with living below the privilege You have granted to us as Your heirs, and we are not willing to sell out to compromise! The façade that has been built in an attempt to hide the fullness of Your power and Person is now crumbling as the waters of revival are springing forth, and Your Glory shall be revealed.

Jesus, Your true Church is rising and returning to a passionate pursuit of You. We are refocusing on You. Oh, God, we realize the value of Your awesome presence. We cry out for more of You. We listen to and follow Holy Spirit, allowing Him to position us with understanding, wisdom, and revelation coming from the deepest parts of You. We will not stop short of the glory!

Our righteous King Jesus has left us a weapon, a quick and powerful sword to defeat the opposition of the devil and his attempts to stop us. By faith, we take hold of that sword and set our faces like a flint to gaze upon the One who calls us His own.

Our ears are attentive to Your voice. It's time to go forward! It's time for action! We hear the call, and we respond with courageous faith to go beyond what we have known. We will ride with Your strength and power as You send us forth with an already assured victory. We yield ourselves completely to You. May we, as living building stones, find our place in Your plan and become a habitation for You, a temple through which You can reveal Your power and glory.

In Jesus' name, amen!

SECTION THREE

— 12 —

GOD'S VERDICT FOR THE UNITED STATES OF AMERICA

The purposes of God for the United States of America are not a lost cause. The moment we are in has not taken God by surprise. One may be tempted to look through the eyes of the flesh and declare, "America is too far gone!" Such is not the case. God's plan is never at the mercy of what the enemy is doing, nor is God on the defense, trying to gain the victory. The victory was already won as Jesus conquered death, hell, and the grave and ascended triumphantly to the right hand of the Father. His victory has become our victory. We are not seeking to *gain* victory over the plots and schemes of this evil agenda set in place to destroy America; we have *already* been given the victory. We are rising with faith *in* God to occupy what we have been given and continue the triumph of the ages.

The Church is being called to attention and to their post to be God's voice, releasing His verdicts that will reconnect this nation with His heart and desires. This is not the time for intimidation or retreat. It's time for the Church, the Body of Christ, to stand securely and confidently with faith in God, unshaken in our expectation and persuasion that the good work He has begun in this nation, He is faithful to complete.

The dreams in this section of the book reveal the verdict of God for our nation and the unfolding call for the Body of Christ to rise with boldness and unrelenting resolve to be light shining in the darkness, making Christ known. These dreams also reveal the intended outcome that God desires—awakening and transformation. God has remembered His promises, and many of those promises for another great awakening have now embarked upon their prophetic timing, and God is now watching over His Word to perform it.

RIDE THE WAVE

There is a temptation among many in the Church to relegate a move of God just to what happens inside our buildings. However, a real move of God will extend far beyond our gatherings, as a wave of unstoppable power changing the culture, shifting governments, uncovering cures for major diseases, and changing the moral, spiritual, governmental, and economic standings and atmospheres of regions, states, and nations. A real move of God will leave people with the indisputable realization that Yahweh is God and that beside Him there is no other!

A real move of God is initiated by God through the lives of believers who are completely His. They have eyes for only Him. Their ears are attentive to His leading, and they march to the rhythm of His sound. They move with His agenda to decree and enforce His verdicts. They are in marketplaces, schools, businesses, and influential places. They are doctors, nurses, lawyers, politicians, teachers, professors, actors, reporters, police officers, and firefighters. They are technicians, inventors, seamstresses, artists, sports figures, garbage collectors, painters, carpenters—every profession. God has people strategically placed in *thousands* of positions that span the globe.

They are not just there for a job. They are vessels through which Jehovah will reveal His wisdom, power, glory, and might. They are on assignment, and wherever they go they release the river of God that brings life. They carry "fire power." They carry the purposes of God, and they are anointed to continue what Jesus taught and did. They are positioned with an ability through Christ to release the sound of triumph into our nation and our world. The time has come for the revealing of the fullness of God through these Kingdom advancers.

Awakening revival will be felt and experienced within the Church, but it won't stop there. God is provoking His people to move past the soulish realm of human ideas and even past some of the "prophetic" expressions and "spiritual giftings" that have become more of an entertainment than a true demonstration of the life-changing glory of God. Spiritual giftings are not given so we become enamored with those who operate in them!

The Church does not exist for the sole purpose of merely tending to sheep. His gifts are real and church gatherings are necessary, but His desire for both is not to appease the flesh, but rather through them that He may transform our lives and impart to us strategy and wisdom and awaken in us true courageous faith, enabling us to take our place as equipped ambassadors for Christ and His righteous cause.

A real move of God is now beginning, and it will be demonstrated on levels unfamiliar within the Church! It is bigger, far greater than anything we've ever known. This move of God is putting a demand on the true Church to rise, think outside the box, listen for His instructions, and *be* the Body of Christ! He wants to give us creative ideas, solutions to unresolved problems, cures for diseases, and supernatural ability to represent Him as He works through us with undeniable power that will impact the culture in such a way that it awakens hearts to an awareness of Him.

I heard the Lord say,

> *You are about to ride the crest of the wave. (The crest is the point of greatest upward thrust in a wave.) You are at the point of final displacement of all that would hold you back. This is the point of no return! It's the point of total commitment. There can be no compromise! It is the place where you become completely Mine. It is the point of greatest surrender and trust. It is total dependency and sensitivity to Christ, alone. Like Peter walking on the water, as long as you're focused on Me, you will go where you have never gone and do what you have never done!*
>
> *Hold on! The tide is rising! Many have been playing in the water. They think they know what a wave feels like—and maybe they do, somewhat—but this is not that. A wave has formed that eyes have not seen. You have never passed this way before. This is the place of total trust in Me. Will you ride?*
>
> *The wave has formed, but it's still rising. Don't abandon your stand of focus and faith. Do not give in to fear of the turbulent rising! Stay focused in the rising. Stay humble, and stay focused on Me.*
>
> *Listen for My voice. Watch in the Spirit. The rise and the crest are near, and My committed ones will be suddenly thrust into a place of great decision and opportunity for great effectiveness. This is your greatest hour. Don't shrink back; stay the course. Do not fear humankind! Do not fear the wave. Get above it and ride the wave in the power of My glory! What is meant for evil, I will turn for good!*

We have entered a new era. We've never passed this way before; therefore, we must keep our eyes on Jesus. We must stand steadfast on the Word of God and be led by the Spirit of God. History is ready to be made.

The crest of the wave is forming.

Will you ride?

— 13 —

AMERICA SHALL BE SAVED

In 2018 I had a very significant dream. I had no idea at the time how God would use this dream to literally be part of shifting the prayer movement in this nation. It was an announcement from Heaven to reveal God's heart and intentions for the United States. Its message would give the Ekklesia hope and strategy for the future into which we were being ushered.

> In the dream, I, along with two fellow intercessors and my mom and dad, were walking down Pennsylvania Avenue in Washington, DC. I knew the Turnaround Conference at the Trump Hotel was just ending at that very moment. (This was an actual conference held at the Trump Hotel a couple of weeks *after* I had this dream. It was a gathering of national and international intercessors who had come to Washington, DC. for the sole purpose of making an appeal to Heaven on behalf of the United States of America.)
>
> In the dream, as we were on Pennsylvania Avenue, we turned and saw a courier angel coming outside through the doors of the Trump Hotel where the conference was just

ending. This angel was carrying a fairly large scroll. His face was set toward the United States Capitol Building, and he was heading immediately in that direction. We decided to follow him as he went into the Capitol. We then entered into the House Chamber, and the scene was exactly as it had been at the State of the Union address given by President Donald Trump just a few nights prior to this dream. All of the lawmakers were there in their seats, and there were many people in the gallery. It was a packed house.

The courier angel with the scroll was standing at the double doors leading into the House Chamber, and he loudly announced with authority and confidence, "ALL RISE!" And just as had happened at the previous State of the Union Address, some people stood, while others disrespectfully and very snidely stayed seated.

The angel then opened the scroll and said very loudly and adamantly, "The verdict has been determined: AMERICA SHALL BE SAVED!"

Immediately a cloud, the glory of God, came from behind the angel and began to fill the room. Those who had stood at his entrance were now crumpled to their knees, wailing, broken by the reality of God's presence. Two or three others, who had been seated before, were now on their knees, screaming out very loudly, "I'm sorry! I'm *so sorry*!" while others remained seated.

I knew in that moment that judgment was beginning to be administered and that God's ruling authority was being set in place. It was transformation and reformation being established for America's new reality: *She shall be saved!*

And that was the end of the dream.

In the dream, my fellow intercessors and I were walking with my mom and dad. The dream also included a meeting in which intercessors had gathered from all across the nation and other parts of the world. This gives us a picture of the necessity of the joining of the generations and also of the importance of fervent, intentional intercession that was key in bringing about the response from Heaven, God's verdict for the nation.

GOD'S VERDICT

Prayer is a vital part of awakening and revival. Effectual, fervent prayer is not a last-minute attempt to somehow, hopefully get God to involve Himself in our situations. Effectual, fervent prayer comes from the heart of confidence and faith that has been established from abiding in the Lord's presence.

I think of Moses, as he was leading the people of Israel to possess the land that God had promised. The promise was real and certain, but there had to be obedience to follow God as He led them into its fulfillment. As they journeyed, there were times when Moses would take a tent and pitch it outside the camp. He called it "the tent of meeting." He would go there to seek the Lord, and God would meet with him in that tent.

The Bible says that God spoke to Moses *"face to face, as one speaks to a friend"* (Exodus 33:11 NIV). Moses sought the Lord, and he heard the strategies of Heaven that enabled him to lead the people. It was in one of those "meetings" with the Lord where Moses received God's assurance that His presence would go with them and He would give them rest. God sealed it with this promise: *"I will do this thing that you have spoken; for you have found grace in My sight, and I know you by name"* (Exodus 33:17 NKJV).

As mentioned before, an actual prayer meeting took place at the Trump Hotel in Washington, DC in February 2018. For a few days, that hotel served as a "tent of meeting," as thousands in person and via the Internet gathered to make a fervent appeal to Heaven on behalf of the United States of America. The dream revealed that those prayers set things into motion. God heard their cry and responded with a verdict that still rings true for our nation today: "America shall be saved!" This is not a cute catch phrase; this is a verdict rendered by God Himself, and it is a promise that will be fulfilled by the God Who made it. What will save America is an awakening to God. God has spoken, and He has sealed it with the promise, *"I will do this thing!"*

Each of us has a part in God's plan to fulfill this promise and enforce His verdict. Each of us has our purpose in God. Our purpose is not defined by what others are called to be and do. We are not in competition, and to compare ourselves among ourselves is not wise! We are who God says we are, and we are anointed to do what God has created us to do. Everyone has purpose, but however God chooses to work through us, the end goal is always the same. He works in us and through us as He will so that Christ will be seen and made known. Attached to the purpose is the responsibility to seek God and allow Him to work through us.

We see in this dream the joining of the generations—young and old, walking together, focused on and devoted to God, attentive to Holy Spirit to hear and obey His leading. Through us God's will can be done and His Kingdom can come.

TAKE YOUR PLACE

I want to interject something here that I think is crucial. I want to speak to the older generation and exhort you to take your place. God is not finished with you! Though there is a church culture now that caters almost entirely to the needs and desires of the youth in an attempt to draw them into our buildings, we must never neglect to honor and glean from the wisdom carried by many seasoned "generals of the faith," who have spent their lives seeking and walking with God, gaining valuable experience and understanding that is still beneficial for us today.

The following dream paints a clear picture of the necessity of joining the generations.

> In the dream, I was standing under a tree in front of an old, two-story historical home. There was a beautiful wrap-around porch, and sitting on that porch were seven generals, including George Washington and two women. I knew they were generals because they were wearing uniforms with their medals and stars.
>
> Each general was sitting in a rocking chair. Some of them had walkers in front of them; others had a walking cane hanging on their chair.
>
> I saw George Washington get up, and with his cane he walked over to a table that was situated beside the door of the house. He looked down and carefully studied some papers lying on the table. Then he returned to his rocking chair.
>
> I somehow knew that each general was thinking, *There's more fight left in me! I'm not done!* Yet their heads hung down and they just sat there rocking in their chairs.

On the lawn in front of them were hundreds of younger people speaking to the generals. There comments included, "We've got this! You've trained us, and you can just sit there and retire. We don't need you now. We can do this without you."

Way out in front of this house, I could see a major battle taking place—one such as in the Revolutionary or Civil War. The generals were looking out at the battle and thinking, *There's more fight left in me!*

But the crowd of young people had convinced the generals it was best and safer for them to stay seated on the porch while the younger group went out to deal with the battle. They continued to say, "We've got this. We can do it without you! Just stay here and be safe."

Behind the younger crowd was a fence, and beyond that fence was yet another group of people, who were trying to get a message through to the generals, but the younger crowd wouldn't allow it.

This other crowd wanted to tell the generals, "We can't get through *that* (pointing to the battle) without you! We need you to lead us through that! There are two more battles beyond that one, and these (referring to that younger crowd) don't know the strategies well enough to lead us through."

For the generals to hear their message, some started getting on the shoulders of others so their voices could be heard over the younger crowd. They were shouting to the generals, "We need you to take your place and lead us! These don't know yet how to lead us! They have the abilities (meaning the physical strength), but they don't know the strategies!"

Finally, George Washington heard the other people, and he looked up. He cupped his hands around his ears so he could hear more clearly what they were saying. Someone then shouted to him, "Look beside you! *You* have the battle plans!" He looked down beside him, and there were two rolled-up parchments. Each parchment was maybe two and a half or three feet tall and had precise, detailed battle plans drawn on them.

He instructed the other generals to listen to what those people were saying. Each cupped their hands behind their ears and heard the people say, "Look beside you! *You* have the battle plans!" And each general noticed two rolled-up parchments beside them. Each set of parchments contained the same strategies, and each general *had* the strategies.

George Washington said, "We have to get up and do something with these battle plans." All the generals rose to their feet.

One asked, "How do we do this?"

Washington stepped to the edge of the porch and spoke to everyone there "We have to combine our efforts!" Then he addressed the younger crowd, "You are deceived if you think you can do this without us." These words were not spoken in arrogance, but more as a warning. He held up the parchments and said, "These are the battle plans, and none of us can do anything without these plans. But you don't yet know how to 'govern' the plans."

All of the generals took their parchments containing the plans and walked over to the table beside the door—the same table George Washington had walked over to at the beginning of the dream. I then realized that the papers on the table he had been studying were the same battle plans drawn on the parchments.

Then each general unfurled their parchments, and all the people—both the younger crowd and those beyond the fence—came together as one unit and moved closer to the porch. Using those plans, the generals began to "govern" the people. They left their walkers, canes, and rocking chairs behind and were ready to share God's battle plans. New life came forth from them as they realized they were still valued and needed. They stayed on the porch, but they led the people with strategies to gain victory in the battle they could see and also in the two battles yet to come.

That was the end of the dream.

To those among the older generation who have felt pushed to the side as though your time has come and gone and you have no place or part in the awakening revival beginning to unfold, I hear the Lord saying, *"This is not the time for you to sit back in your rocking chairs, waiting to graduate to Heaven. There is more fight left in you. It is time for you to rise and shine with the light of wisdom that has come by way of your experiences with Me that will lead a generation in and to victory."*

Speaking on behalf of my generation and those younger than I, I say to those among us who have paid the price and who have believed the promises of God and who have run with the assignments that have led us to this defining moment, *we need you!* We can't do this without you!

We need your wisdom, experience, and guidance. Tell us your stories. Tell us what you have learned. Tell us what you have done. Tell us what you have experienced. You are the libraries of wisdom and knowledge that we need.

SPIRITUAL TRUTHS AND STRATEGIES

There are truths and spiritual strategies we can and must gain from those who have journeyed ahead of us. It's not that we allow past truth to tie us to the hitching post of what God has done, but we must have knowledge of past truth to help guide us into true present revelation. This knowledge enables us to successfully advance into the fullness of God's purposes and intentions for this moment and to enforce His verdicts and carry out His present assignments with victory.

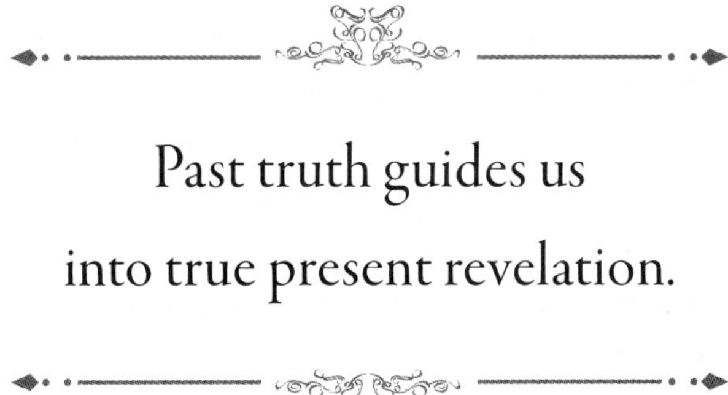

Past truth guides us into true present revelation.

That is not to say the younger generations have no relevant wisdom or ability to advance the Kingdom or to lead others. There *are* many who have been as Elisha as he walked with Elijah. They have watched, listened, and learned from mature leaders through whom God worked to lead them. They have caught the mantle that launched them into the manifested power of God, allowing them experiences that are giving them confidence in God and maturing them in their callings (see 2 Kings 2:1-15). You, too, are needed. Your strength and courageous faith and obedience to God are vitally necessary as we advance. We are one Body, and every part of the Body of Christ must do its part!

Joining the generations means we are rising together to take our place on the timeline of history. Together we will contend for and see this awakening that was prophesied for our day. We are uniting in our faith in God. We link arms and lock shields, and we advance in victory! Yes, we see the distress in our nation and in our world, but we are not deterred by the battles that may rage around us. God has a plan, and He is giving us strategies to see to it that every part of His plan is fulfilled. Hell cannot stop what God has started, and hell cannot prevail against the Church Jesus has built.

God has awakened the watchmen, young and old, and He has called us to be His representatives and His mouthpieces, releasing His Word with His authority to set necessary things into motion. Holy Spirit is beginning to announce in detail things that are to come. He is giving us strategies for the warfare confronting us. This is a spiritual warfare, so we must lean heavily on Holy Spirit and allow Him to impart to us God's wisdom for the days ahead. Intercession is a key component to the reality of this awakening.

America's future will largely be impacted by the people of prayer, who have learned to see *beyond*. It will be impacted by those sold-out prayer warriors, who stand guard on the walls of this nation to hear what God is saying and declare and enforce what Holy Spirit reveals from the mind and mouth of God.

God's ruling authority has been set in place. Transformation and reformation have been prophesied, and God has instructed His governing body to move with boldness and confidence, with the backing of His might and power, to shine with the light of His manifested glory, and release the decrees to enforce His verdict: *"America shall be saved!"*

Let's pray:

> *Father, we see and know that we are riding the crest of the wave—the wave of destiny, the wave of the move of Holy Spirit in our time. We feel the thrust of the increasing momentum, but we will not give in to fear of the turbulent rising. We will remain in a position of focus and faith in You.*
>
> *We humble ourselves to seek Your face and to receive Your strategies. You will release those strategies to us by way of Your Word and by supernatural revelation given by Holy Spirit. You will also utilize the experiences of those who have faithfully walked with You through the years to help enlighten us with necessary wisdom and understanding for our advancement. We resist pride that suggests we know how to move forward without the wisdom and knowledge of those who have a lifetime of experiences with You. We link arms together and lock our shields, young and old, and we advance as the Church You have built, against which the gates of hell cannot prevail.*
>
> *Lord, You have heard the cries of the generations—and now the cries of those in our times—and You have responded to those sincere appeals with Your determined verdict: "America* ***shall*** *be saved!" And we rise with an unquenchable resolve to move with You and for You to see Your will happen in our nation! We declare the downfall and annihilation of every scheme and plot of hell sent to change laws and times to throw this nation off its God-ordained*

course and destiny! We declare that those snares are broken! Those plots and schemes meet with a defeated end! Hell will not prevail against Church, and hell will not prevail against Your original plans and intentions for the United States!

You have determined and declared that America shall be saved! And we, as Your legislative body, Your united Ekklesia, now declare that verdict with the backing of Your might and authority. We speak Your Word, and You will watch over that Word to perform the doing of it!

It is so...in Jesus' name!

Amen.

— 14 —

AWAKENING AMERICA

In many of the dreams I have shared thus far, God is obviously revealing to us that He has His eye on the United States of America. He has targeted us for the spearhead of another greater awakening to manifest in our time. Each state in this nation has purpose. Each state has a remnant believing God, cooperating with Holy Spirit, and declaring the intentions of God into their atmosphere to set into motion the purposes of God for their regions, territories, and state.

Now, God is pulling it all together. Like pieces of a puzzle, the picture is beginning to come into view—a picture of revival fire burning in and transforming our nation.

Another great awakening *is* unfolding. God *is* saving America! We know that He has not forsaken His promises. *"From eternity to eternity I Am God. No one can snatch anyone out of My hand. No one can undo what I have done"* (Isaiah 43:13 NLT). He is powerful and mighty to save! (See Zephaniah 3:17.)

We know and believe that God is working, but we must realize that He, more often than not, works through His people to accomplish His desired will. So as we shout our decrees and agreement with God's prophetic promises, and believe Him for the fulfillment of those promises, we must never take our obedience to Him out of the equation. Our most important posture in this defining moment is the posture of prayer *and* obedience to God. As we humble ourselves to walk with the Lord and yield to Holy Spirit's leading, God will reveal to us His thoughts and intentions—keys of wisdom to advance with effectiveness and success as His witnesses. The following dream gives a profound illustration of this truth.

HE IS GIVING US THE KEYS

I dreamed I was with a team of intercessors, and we were riding on a tour bus, driving across a bridge leading to an old castle. We could see it in the distance as we drove toward it. We arrived at the front of the castle and instantly felt a very strong presence of the Lord. There were huge, stone steps leading up to the entrance of the castle. The team walked up the steps, and a man there greeted us and told us why we were at this place. He said, "You have tasks in front of you—things you need to do. When you complete each task, you will receive the key to unlock your next task."

The man then opened the two very large wooden doors, and we could see inside the castle. There was a very long hallway with several doors on each side. The man gave us a key and said, "You'll find your first task in this room." He pointed toward the door nearest to us in the hallway. We used the key to unlock the door and went into the room.

(Throughout the dream, there were eight rooms we went into. Each room had a specific task we were to accomplish, but I can't yet remember every task.)

In the first room we entered, there was a very large painting of a heart on the wall—not a physical, anatomical heart, but like the hearts we draw as the symbol of love. It was a beautiful painting, and we were all amazed and captivated by the artistic ability of the painter. Our task or assignment in this room was to pray until we knew what was on God's heart.

There remained an overwhelming awareness of the presence of the Lord. The Spirit of the Lord was hovering over this entire place. The whole team fell on our knees, and we began to pray in the Spirit. We were all crying—not sad, just so aware of His presence.

One of our team members began to sob with deep groaning. When he could speak, he said, "I know what's on God's heart. God gave me His heart for this. It's America. America is on God's heart." We all were so deeply moved by this realization, and we fervently began to cry out for America.

As we prayed, we saw an American flag emerge from the heart in the painting. The heart was a painting, but the flag was real. It unfurled and began to wave as though waving in the wind. When that happened, a key fell onto the floor, and we knew our task in this room had been accomplished. We took the key and went into the next room.

I don't remember our assignment in that room, but we came out with our next key and continued down the hallway to another room.

In this room, the man who had greeted us at the front of the castle was there. He said, "Your task now is to put this puzzle together." He was holding a wooden box that contained puzzle pieces. He opened the box and poured the pieces onto a table that was in the center of the room. We realized the puzzle pieces were in the shape of states—each of the fifty states of the USA.

We put the pieces together, forming a map of the United States of America. Then we saw on each piece, each state, a Scripture reference we were to declare and pray into for each individual state. I don't remember any of the references, but each state had one. So we declared these verses over the states; and when we were finished, the key to the next room fell onto the table on top of the puzzle.

I only remember the tasks from a couple of other rooms, but I know that we completed the task in each room and received the keys for the next assignments.

In the seventh room we entered, we found a long wooden church pew sitting in the middle of the floor. The man was there in this room, and He said, "I am now going to *open* your heart for My movement in America, and I'm going to put a *passion* into your hearts for My movement in America."

That's when we knew the man was actually the Lord.

On that church pew, items appeared, one at a time. The first to appear was the stump of a tree. We asked the Lord what this was, and He said, *"From this stump, one of the ministers declared My Word during the revival at Red River."*

The next to appear on the pew were two charred logs that were crisscrossed. The Lord said, *"These are from the fires at Cane Ridge."*

The next item looked like a thick, square paper bag or a box. He said, *"This is what William Seymour put over his head when he would pray before the meetings at Azusa. It still contains those prayers of William Seymour. I haven't forgotten those prayers."*

Then a hymnal appeared. He said, *"This hymnal contains the songs that were written and the Psalms that were joyfully sung to Me in the revival in the Hebrides."*

Then there was a pair of forearm crutches (the kind that strap onto the forearm and has the short pieces to hold on to). The Lord said, *"These are from My healing movement with John G. Lake."* He then told us the story of the man who used those crutches and how he was healed.

Next, I saw a Bible appear on the pew. The Lord said, *"This Bible belonged to Kenneth Hagin (Kenneth E. Hagin). It contains the notes of the revelations I gave to him."*

The Lord then instructed our team to gather the things on the pew and take them with us. He said, *"You cannot proceed in My movement forward without honoring the movement of what I've done before. It's all one movement...My movement."*

At this point, the entire team was on the floor, and someone began to pray, paraphrasing from Habakkuk 3:2, saying, *"O Lord, we have heard of You and of Your work, and we have reverence for You. Lord, in the midst of our years, revive this work and even greater. Make Your power and presence known in our times."* We all agreed and began to pray this prayer together. Then the next key appeared on the pew, we took it and moved to the final room, carrying with us all of the items revealed to us from the past moves of God.

In the last room, there was a huge Bible laying on a table. The Bible was opened to the book of Hosea. Our assignment was to read this book. Many on the team took turns stepping up to the table and reading aloud from Hosea. Some read a few verses, and others read a whole chapter.

As we were doing this, the Lord stepped out from a corner in the room. It was then that although He had only made Himself known in a few of the rooms, I now knew He had been present in every room. And here in this room, we were all *very* aware of His presence.

When He stepped out from the corner of the room, He said, *"I love America, but she is far away from Me. You see it here in Hosea."* We all nodded our heads in agreement that we could definitely see it in those Scriptures. He continued, *"But, I love her, and I've determined her salvation."* We were all weeping, just *so* overwhelmed by His presence and with the passion of His heart for America that He had put in our hearts.

At this time I could see a portion of the book entitled *Rees Howells Intercessor*. The book was not there, but I could see it so clearly as though it were. The portion of the book I saw was from the thirty-second chapter, which gives an eyewitness account of a time in 1934 when these intercessors had a life-changing encounter with the Lord. The Holy Spirit moved among them in very powerful ways for several days on the campus of Rees Howell's college. (Having read this book several times, this chapter has always captivated me as I would read of this account. So, in the dream, though I couldn't recite word for word what was written in the book, I knew and was very familiar with what I was seeing.) Our entire team was deeply impacted by what we saw, heard, and had encountered in this room.

Before we left there, the Lord gave to one of our team members what we thought was a single key, and He then led us out of the castle. We walked through another set of large wooden doors onto a porch. We saw a drawbridge being lowered over a moat. Just then, a massive wave of water began to move, not just through the moat, but it also went out from there into the entire nation.

On the other side of the drawbridge were saddled horses, one for each of us. That's when we realized that the Lord had not just given us a single key, but a ring that contained all of the eight keys we had received from the completed assignments.

> Then a strong wind began to blow, and the Lord said to us, *"The time has come for You to ride in the wind and declare My salvation to America...and I've given you the keys."*
>
> We walked across the drawbridge, mounted the horses, and rode out from there.

That was the end of the dream.

The castle in this dream represents, to me, the revelatory realm of the Spirit. The bus that brought us to this place was filled with intercessors, which reveals we enter this realm by way of prayer. We know that Jesus is the only way to God (see John 14:6 NKJV). By receiving Jesus as Lord of our lives through salvation, we have been given access to know God as Father. And as His born-again children, we may now *"come boldly to the throne of grace"* (Hebrews 4:16 NKJV).

We can pray, and He will hear us (see Jeremiah 29:12-13). We can draw near to Him, and He will draw near to us (see James 4:8). And as we worship Him and humble ourselves to pray, we access His presence, the realm of revealed revelation, where we can hear His direction, receive His strategies, and know what is on His mind.

He shares with us, by Holy Spirit, the deepest parts of His heart so we can know the things He has freely given to us (see 1 Corinthians 2:10, 12). And knowing His will, we can then move with His wisdom and might to accomplish His purposes. This is how Jesus operated in His earthly life. He was a man of prayer, and by entering into the presence of the Father, He could see what God wanted Him to do (see John 5:19). Knowing God's will enabled Him to know what to say and to do in every situation He faced.

THE WILL OF GOD

God invites us to come into His presence to see and to know His will. Knowing the will of God builds faith and confidence to trust and follow His leading. It's the difference between being told to go on a journey and being given an address for where you're going. You may not know all of the turns and means of getting there, but when you know where you're going, that information gives you the ability to navigate and arrive there successfully.

The insights we receive from God in prayer become keys of revelation that will unlock necessary components to successfully navigate the journey ahead. Armed with these keys, we can then ride with the wind of Holy Spirit, Who empowers us to accomplish the purposes for which God is sending us.

Also, in this dream, God once again reveals to us the value of knowing, honoring, and celebrating what He has done in the generations before us. Those amazing past moves of God actually contribute greatly to the continuation of His plans for our times. The testimony of His past faithfulness and the undeniable fruit of the manifestation of His power prophesy to us that what He has done, He is able and willing to do again—and even greater if we walk with Him in faith and obedience.

God reveals His love, and He reveals what are hindrances to the full manifestation of His power. The answer to what is happening in our nation and in our world today is not found in government, media, or human abilities. The answer is a genuine encounter with God in the power of His Spirit.

I believe the Church is entering such an encounter—the place of total transformation that brings us to the place of being completely His, the place where we put on Christ and emerge as Christ-like warriors anointed to ride with the wind of Holy Spirit and see the salvation of the Lord as He moves through us to reform the nation and turn hearts back to Him.

— 15 —

INTERSTATE 40 DREAMS

I have had very significant dreams focused on Interstate 40 that runs across the breadth of the United States, from North Carolina to California. In each of these dreams I felt that I-40 was also referring to Isaiah 40. While I'm sure there are very significant revelations in these dreams that have to do with specific areas along this interstate, I also feel it is important for us to look at some key verses from Isaiah 40 to gain deeper insight into God's intentions for these dreams.

The following stood out to me in Isaiah 40:

1. "'Comfort, yes, comfort My people!' says your God" (Isaiah 40:1 NKJV).

Holy Spirit is the Comforter (John 14:16), and while this verse may address the actual comfort that was experienced in the hearts of the people of Jerusalem as they heard the words of the Lord that *"her warfare is ended, her iniquity is pardoned"* (Isaiah 40:2), I believe this verse also points us to a reference of the operation of Holy Spirit, our great Comforter, Whom Jesus sent back to earth after His ascension. Without doubt, one of the major components of this great awakening will be the manifestation of the undeniable peace and supernatural, tangible comfort of Holy Spirit that will overtake the hearts of those who are surrendered to God. Though chaos and deep uncertainties trouble the minds of many in the world, by the power of our Comforter, we can remain calm and unshaken. The evidence of Christ's peace upon us will be an unavoidable witness speaking volumes to those around us who are ensnared by anxiety and fear.

2. "The glory of the Lord shall be revealed, and all flesh shall see it together; for the mouth of the Lord has spoken" (Isaiah 40:5 NKJV).

The mouth of the Lord has spoken it. *"The grass withers, the flower fades, but the word of our God stands forever"* (verse 8). He speaks with intent to perform—so America, get ready! An unstoppable, unavoidable wave of the glory of God is going to sweep across this land. The fire of God, the manifested demonstration of God's power and glory will be revealed. It has already begun.

3. To the Ekklesia, the Body of Christ, He says it's time to find your voice and cry out.

We are His witnesses, and He is renewing and increasing our strength so we can "*mount up with wings like eagles*" (Isaiah 40:29-31 NKJV) and run with His message of truth and triumph. Don't hold back. Release the sound of the voice of triumph.

> *You herald of good tidings! Make the news ring out! Don't be afraid! Say to these cities...'Behold your God!' The Lord, the Eternal, comes with power, with unstoppable might;*

> *He will take control without question or delay. He will see to it that wages are paid, repairs are made, and all is set right again* (Isaiah 40:9-10 VOICE).

I encourage you to take time to read all of Isaiah chapter 40 in your Bible and allow Holy Spirit to reveal more truths and key insights to you from these verses and concerning the following dreams.

"NOW...<u>THIS</u> IS MY AMERICA"

In a dream:

> I was lifted up, and I saw the United States of America. I wasn't seeing a paper map, I was looking down upon the whole nation. I saw it all, including Hawaii and Alaska.
>
> My attention was drawn to Interstate 40. I saw Dutch Sheets (an apostle) and Chuck Pierce (a prophet), standing side by side on I-40 where it begins in North Carolina. Dutch and Chuck were like two matches, and their heads were like the tips of the matches. (I don't know how to explain that exactly.)
>
> I then saw the hand of the Lord come down and take the apostle and the prophet and pull them across the entire length of I-40, east to west, like a match being pulled across a rough surface to be lit.
>
> When they reached California, the "matches" ignited, and immediately a fire was lit that spread up the entire

West Coast, from top to bottom, even into Alaska. It also included the Hawaiian Islands.

The fire then began to spread as one long line of a rolling wave back toward the East Coast. It was moving very slowly at first. As it moved, I noticed that in front of the wave of fire the land looked charred in many spots, like a destructive fire had previously burned there. But as *this* wave of fire moved across it, the charred land actually became lush and green.

Then I saw large solar panels popping up in various locations behind the wave of fire as it moved across the land. Again, it was moving slowly. But when it reached the center of the nation, about even with the border between Texas and Louisiana, I saw an opening forming on the southern coast between those two states. A massive wind began to blow through that opening. The wind went with force straight up the middle of the country behind the wave of fire. The wind then began to thrust the fire forward at a much more rapid pace. Now, the fire was *racing* toward the East Coast. I could see oil drilling platforms and pumps, windmills, and more solar panels popping up behind the fire, and I heard the Lord announce, *"This is **My** 'renewing' energy! I Am energizing America!"*

The fire wave, still being pushed by the wind, made it to the East Coast. What was unfolding behind the fire wave had been creating a picture. I couldn't see what the finished picture looked like, but the edge of the picture was folded under, and the edge of the nation on the East Coast was folded upward. The two edges were then lapped over each

> other and connected, and I saw a hand come down and lock them into place. I then heard the Lord say, *"Now...**this** is **My** America."*

And that was the end of the dream.

RUN WITH THE FIRE

In another dream:

> I saw a runner positioned in starting blocks, and then he began to run. His "starting line" was on Interstate 40 at the North Carolina and Tennessee border.
>
> The runner was moving at a supernatural pace. He was running across America, going west on Interstate 40. He was running so fast that his feet were on fire, and he was leaving a trail of fire behind him. And the fire never went out.
>
> He ran to the end of I-40, and when he reached California, he turned left toward the city of Los Angeles. When he reached a "specific" location, I could see that the runner was Dutch Sheets. He had a number pinned on his chest: #8. The "specific" location he had reached was the site of the Azusa Street Revival.
>
> At this place was a geyser of both fire and water shooting from the ground and into the air. This reminded me of the geyser I saw in the Red River Meeting House dream.

Dutch literally stepped into the geyser and was saturated with water, and he was carrying fire all about him when he emerged. Facing eastward, he bent over slightly, cupped his hands on either side of his mouth, and with everything inside of him, he yelled very long and very loudly one word: "F-I-I-I-R-R-R-E!" He was declaring this over the nation.

Instantly, the sound he released was amplified, and it was rolling out in waves and waves of power all across America—across all fifty states. (I didn't see this in all of the states, but I knew it was happening from the West Coast into the nation!)

Dutch then made his way back to Interstate 40 and started running eastward. I could see the fire was still burning where he had previously run on the westbound side of I-40. As he ran, his feet were still ablaze, and he was still leaving a trail of fire behind him, but now he was also leaving a trail of the water he had been saturated with at the Azusa Street location.

As he ran eastward on I-40, he stopped at five strategic locations. (I don't remember them all, but I specifically remember that two of the locations were somewhere near Tulsa, Oklahoma, and somewhere in Memphis, Tennessee, near the Mississippi River.)

At each of the five locations, Dutch stood before a crowd of people, still saturated with water and his feet still on fire. He released very strong decrees and declarations from Isaiah, chapter 40. As he did this, the fire and water he carried were being released onto the people.

> He ran the entire length of I-40, leaving the trail of fire and water as he went.

That's all I can remember of the dream.

REVELATION FOR THE I-40 DREAMS

God has a great plan for this great nation, and it's time to unfold another part of that plan. Through these dreams, we clearly see His intentions to reform, realign, and reestablish America, bringing Her back on track with His original intentions for Her existence. There is a massive move of God that will energize the Body of Christ and bring a reviving and restoration to this nation that will once again display God's idea of what America should be. He is at work even now.

Within the country, there are many states, and within the states there are many cities and regions, each carrying their own prophetic destiny that contributes to God's purposes for the nation as a whole. Within those states, cities, and regions, God has strategically placed people who carry necessary purpose for this time for those locations.

To those within the states and cities specifically named in these dreams, I suggest you seek the Lord for strategy and pray for revelation of the specific plans of God for your region, city, or state. These locations are being targeted by the Lord, and an anointing is being released that will cause your prayers, declarations, and obedience to push back against the darkness as the might of God is released through you.

California, the Lord says to you, *"You are an unseen treasure that will be brought to light in the days ahead. Many will come to you and 'discover' valuable resources that will be instrumental for fueling the fires of revival. There is a swell of revival history within your streets that is ready to be released again with an even greater thrust. From south to north the revival fires will ignite, and the winds from the ocean of My love and power will push the fires eastward bringing an awakening of holy awe and reverence for Me everywhere they go."*

Arizona, the Lord says to you, *"I have come to refresh you with the water of My Spirit. I Am unlocking the gates that have held back the river of My glory, and from this desert land, I will now release great swells of Living Water that will cause flash flooding of unstoppable currents of Holy Spirit power that will re-life the nation. What you have seen and tasted in part will now fully manifest. What I do in you will have a grand impact on the nation and nations of the world."*

New Mexico, the Lord says to you, *"I see you! I have heard the cries of your hearts. I will now blow on the small pockets of revival fires that have been ignited in you and create a blaze of glory that will grow as it goes. An acceleration will take place, and I will begin to highlight the hidden ones in this state. Stay on the wall. Stand, and you will see the salvation of the Lord. The desert will bloom again, attracting the attention of many who will be drawn to My glory that shall be revealed in you!"*

Texas, the Lord says to you, *"The release of Holy Spirit power that is set to flow from your borders will generate a great wind of the Spirit, bringing life and reviving. From the depths of your heart will rise a sound that will provoke an unstoppable movement of My Spirit that will bridge the divide and unite the nation. The light of My glory has risen upon you, Texas, and you will shine with that light to expose what has been hidden in the darkness, and you will operate in My wisdom to reinstate truth that will set the nation free."*

Oklahoma, the Lord says to you, *"The delay that has plagued you for the past seasons has been broken, and there is an anointing to release a sooner and not later initiative that will unlock many things that will contribute to the Great Awakening that is now unfolding. The faith foundation that has been laid in you will be instrumental in provoking an uncommon obedience to the leading of My Spirit, serving as an example which others will follow. The shackles of fear and intimidation are being broken from you, and you will become known as 'The Land where Faith Conquers Fear.' I Am making you a testimony of My restoration power and of My transforming glory."*

Arkansas, the Lord says to you, *"You are a diamond that will show forth many facets of My glory. There are many things I have hidden in you that will now rise to the surface to be seen and utilized for My Kingdom purposes. I have unsealed the geyser in the heart of your state, and it will now erupt with supernatural power and demonstrated glory with which I will draw people to your land to discover the value and experience the power of My abiding presence."*

Tennessee, the Lord says to you, *"Out of you will flow a fresh sound of awakening. I Am unlocking that sound even now. I Am raising you up in this hour as a voice and a light to the nation. I Am awakening and mobilizing My volunteer army hidden throughout your land, and they will now run with renewed strength as they receive fresh revelation of My glory. My glory will rise in you and ignite you to shine as a light that enables others to see and be drawn to Me."*

North Carolina, the Lord says to you, *"From your mountains there will be a reviving of My Holy Spirit power that I first poured out there many years ago. That river will flow again with even a greater force. The river comes out of Me, and you must never allow it to be hindered. I Am blowing on the embers of the fire I first ignited there years ago. That fire comes out of Me, and it must never go out. It must ever be burning! The mantle of the evangelist will be dropped on many within your state, and they will run with a fresh urgency as forerunners, bringing the Gospel to the lost and winning many souls to the Kingdom. Fan the flames with your faith-filled prayers and expectation, and you will no longer be a state with revival history—you will be a state that is making revival history. What I do in you will again impact the Church and the nation."*

These are only a few things I have heard as I have prayed over these dreams in which God highlighted these eight states. I exhort you to take these things in consideration and to prayer. Don't stop with this. Listen! The Lord has so much more to reveal.

EIGHT

Another aspect of these dreams that is very important to recognize is the fact that there are eight states, and the number eight was specifically highlighted on the forerunner's jersey who stepped into the fire and water of the opened well at Azusa. The number eight is often indicative of a new beginning. This tells me that God has a remnant scattered throughout these states; and what this remnant does in obedience to His leading is actually contributing to greater things than they may have realized. A launching into a spiritual reality of newness is coming into view. As we work with Holy Spirit and allow Him to work through us, God comes to heal our land. He comes to *"make all things new"* again (Revelation 21:5 NKJV).

So to the remnant in these eight states, and to all of the Ekklesia throughout the USA and the world, rest assured that your labor in the Lord has not been in vain. The remnant is bigger than you can even imagine, and we each carry significant purpose. Now God is beginning to connect the Body, and we will find that our small part becomes greater as it connects to someone else's small part; and as the parts are assembled, there will be an unstoppable, unfathomable flow of glory being revealed.

Wherever you are in America or in the world, find the purpose of God for your life, your region, your state, your nation, and run with it. We find that purpose in Him. As we draw near to Him, Holy Spirit will begin to reveal to us what our eyes haven't seen, our ears haven't heard, and our hearts have never perceived. He is searching out the deepest thoughts of God, and He will impart that wisdom. *"Now we have received, not the spirit of the world, but the Spirit Who is from God"* (1 Corinthians 2:12 NKJV).

So draw near to Him in prayer and worship, and He will impart His wisdom, revelation, and understanding to you. By His Spirit, He will empower you to rise and shine and to run and release the fire of His glory. Colossians 1:27 (NKJV) tells us, *"Christ in you, the hope of glory,"* which is being seen through us!

Recently, the Lord gave me this word to share with the Body of Christ. It is an urgent word that is meant to provoke swift movement from those who have an ear to hear what the Spirit is saying.

> *Today is a day of separation. I Am separating you unto Myself. I Am calling you to engage. Today you must decide, "Will I stay, or will I go?" I Am calling you off the sidelines where you have been comfortable as an uncommitted observer, and I Am positioning you on the frontlines as an all-in warrior. You have said to me, "Heal me, and I'll go." I say to you, "Go! And you will be healed." The healing is in the going.*
>
> *See My fire that is ignited before you, and as did Moses, so you must allow your curiosity to override your comfort and come close*

to Me, and I will speak to you. Come close, and I will consume you. I will reveal My plan for moving forward. I Am not trying to make you comfortable; I Am desiring to make you effective as a burning torch of My glory that lights the way to lead others to Me.

The following word given to me by the Lord several years ago now seems to have met its timing. It is very fitting for the remnant being called to the forefront in this hour. In light of the previous dream, I especially feel this word is very significant for the Church in this nation, and particularly for the Ekklesia positioned within the Gulf Coast States of Texas and Louisiana.

The Lord says:

The wind IS blowing! The Church—not the buildings, but the Body of Christ, those alive and moving with and by My wind—will now arise with gale force as through them I demonstrate My power! This is a point of turning! Stay up in the Spirit! Stand there! Stand still in My presence, and I will fill you afresh with My wind, My Spirit; and I will release you as My whirlwind into this nation, bringing life, My life, to what has seemed dead! Humble yourself. Humble yourself to walk with Me! This IS a point of turning. The wind IS blowing...many changes! Stay in the Spirit so you do not misinterpret the changes and fight against what I will do! You must stay in the Spirit—see and hear in the Spirit—or you will be led by emotions and human interpretation!

I Am now releasing My whirlwinds, and I will blaze an unavoidable trail through this nation that will lead and turn the hearts of many back to Me! Much change will occur in the Church! Many have been lulled to sleep, and they have faded into the shadows of a godless culture! But I will shake, and I will awaken, and I will restore! Align with My order! Get your focus off the culture and focus on Me! Take on My likeness and cast off the conformity of wrong alignment with the culture! You MUST rise above the fray so you can hear! You won't even know what is out of order unless you get up in the Spirit and allow Me to show you My will, My way!

Step into the Wind! Be transformed as I renew you in the wind of My Spirit! I Am breathing on the Body, and you will come alive in My presence! My wind will blow. My gale force wind will blow! Fear not! I have a remnant, and I Am wrapping them in My wind, and they will be My sent ones whom I will release. And with the assistance of Heaven's hosts, they will carry My anointing, clothed in the wind of My Spirit, and through them I will set this nation back on course! It will come with force!

— 16 —

A SET TIME

Fear not, for I am with you; be not dismayed, for I am your God. I will strengthen you, yes, I will help you, I will uphold you with My righteous right hand.

Isaiah 41:10 NKJV

In this set time, the Church has been awakened—maybe not yet as a whole, but at least in part. A remnant has been aroused from slumber, and they rise with a spiritual "knowing" that the time is now! We rise with courageous faith in God and undaunted determination to work with Holy Spirit to see His intentions revive and thrive. We are not in denial of the happenings of our day, but we do not live by what we see—we live by what God has said. God said that America shall be saved! God said we would have another greater move of His Spirit in our time!

Though evil may seem to be prevailing, these things do not move us. We are unshaken from our righteous stand. We believe and know that transformation is coming! We are not given to despair. We are given to fervent prayer, and God *will* heal our land! We release our shouts of triumph, and God is with us to work through us to bring about His prophesied awakening. His declaration to us is, *"Fear not, for I Am with you; be not dismayed, for I Am your God. I will strengthen you, yes, I will help you, I will uphold you with My righteous right hand"* (Isaiah 41:10 NKJV).

We are trailblazers, forerunners, carrying the flame of Yahweh that will initiate awakening in our regions, territories, and states, and the flames of revival are beginning to burn. Never despise small beginnings. The wells of revival have been uncapped, and they are bursting forth with an unstoppable flow. The waters are flammable, causing the nation to be ignited with the flames of awakening. And as we each do our part, releasing our supply, God is now connecting it all, and the nation is being built up as a habitation for Him.

Never underestimate the importance of your acts of obedience to God.

Never underestimate acts of obedience to God. Spend time with Him intentionally, and He will equip you with knowledge of His will, His heart, and His plan. He will connect you with people necessary for your benefit and their benefit as well. He may guide you to places with instruction for necessary prayer assignments. He may guide you to make very specific career choices, give you business or ministry ideas, lead you to run for political office, start a new job, move to a new location, or maybe something as simple as leading you to go to the grocery store when you didn't intend to go, or call a friend you haven't spoken to in years. Whatever the case may be, listen and obey! The people He connects you with may have wisdom or ability to unlock your next assignment—or maybe you are anointed to speak a word to awaken something in *them* that is necessary for *their* journey.

Maybe the prayer assignment will be instrumental in tearing down evil strongholds and shifting the spiritual atmosphere over regions, churches, territories, and will set things in motion to transform lives and spark awakening to God in those regions and territories. Maybe the unplanned visit to the grocery store could lead you to a God-ordained meeting with someone who opens the door you've wanted to open or a door you were not even expecting.

Maybe your run for political office will be the necessary spark that ignites the calling in other people who were afraid to take the leap of faith—and God will begin to transform cities, counties, school districts, states, and even the nation through godly political influencers! Maybe that person He instructs you to call is praying for a specific confirmation from the Lord, and your call is the answer to that prayer. That call could be the key that catapults a major God-happening in and through their lives that will impact many other lives. There is always purpose in His leading.

Holy Spirit will order our steps, and as we obey His leading, He will anoint our feet to run with God's Kingdom purposes, igniting and marking this land with the fires of glory and revival.

Pray from a position of faith in and focus on God. Faith-filled prayer is a powerful weapon that can initiate waves of transforming power. Prayer and obedience to the leading of the Lord being offered by those devoted forerunners, who have submitted their lives to Him with uncompromising dedication, are preparing the way for the King to come.

Now, it's time! The wells are opening, the Ekklesia is uniting, the way is prepared, and we shout to America, *"The King of glory is coming in!"*

The King is making His grand entrance, sparking the greatest awakening to God that this nation and our world have ever known. And everything not of God will become ashes in the wind. What can be shaken will be shaken, and what remains will be what is aligned and functioning in order with God's intentions.

God is moving things out of the way. His plan is in motion, and nothing can stop what He has started! Hidden things are being brought to light. God is ready to expose the hidden operations of hell's agenda. The Church is being called to maintain a position of bold faith and confidence in God to cooperate with Holy Spirit as He leads us. Stay the course. Be bold to run the race God has set before you. Be alert in the Spirit. Oftentimes we find that our simple acts of obedience are blazing a trail for other things to be set into motion, even without our realizing it.

Our focus is not on what our obedience is accomplishing. Our focus is on the Lord. We hear Him, and we obey Him. We live our lives in a conscious awareness of God, attentive to Him. Most of the time, we are not even *trying* to do things. We're just pressing into Him, and part of that pressing is obedience to pray and to fulfill assignments that He gives—great or small. We seek Him first, and as we do, He does through us what we can't do on our own. As we humble ourselves to walk with Him, God is leaving paths of fire behind us that will contribute to this set time of awakening. Be encouraged, things are turning.

Consider the following dream...

THE TURNING PLOW

I dreamed that I was with a group of about two hundred intercessors at the United States Capitol. A split in the ground started to form beginning in front of the Capitol steps and going westward. Everything around us was in chaos, and the city looked like a war zone. Things were out of place and appeared to be in complete upheaval. Suddenly the whole group of us, who were standing there, said in complete unison, "Pray." It wasn't loud. We didn't scream, and it wasn't a fearful thing. It was just a word we released in unison. When we spoke the word "Pray," it seemed to become a wave, a loud roaring wave that went out across the entire nation like a clarion call being sent to the Body of Christ.

Meanwhile, as we stood in front of the Capitol steps, a plow suddenly appeared. It wasn't a tractor plow, but rather an old walk-behind plow made to be pulled by a horse. This type of plow I saw in the dream is called a *turning plow*. The turning plow was *huge,* its tip went deep into the ground, right in front of the Capitol. There was no horse there to pull it, but long ropes were attached to the front of it.

As soon as I noticed it, I walked over to take hold of the handles of the plow. This was all supernatural because in the natural it was so large there was no way I could have even reached the handles. When I took hold of the handles, all the other intercessors came over to the plow. Some of them joined me in taking hold of the handles; others took hold of the ropes and began to pull the plow forward.

At that moment, a host of angels came swooping in to help us. As we moved forward, the plow went deep into that split, breaking open the top of a tunnel hidden beneath the ground.

As the plow was breaking open the tunnel, demons by the thousands came flying up from it. A black cloud formed as the demons boiled out of the ground like a swarm of angry, vicious wasps defending their hiding place that was now being exposed by the plow. The demons were armed with small daggers as they came swarming out of the opened ground. The angels accompanying us fought the demons. The angels were armed with huge swords and were easily defeating the demons. The demons were dropping to the ground and disintegrating.

As we continued to move forward with the giant plow, breaking open the tunnel, the ground continued to split open *ahead of us* like a very ripe watermelon does when you stick a knife in and cut it open. The split just kept going, all the way to the West Coast.

The wave with the roar of the word "pray" that we released at the beginning of the dream was going out in front of us. We could see it. The prayer wave was covering the whole United States of America from top to bottom, and it was moving toward the West Coast. As it moved across certain areas, people would hear the sound and instantly respond to the call to prayer. Some ran into churches and slid on their knees into the altars and prayed. Others fell on their knees in the fields and began to pray. Others ran into houses or businesses—running as fast as they could—and fell to their knees to pray. Hundreds of thousands of people were captured by that wave and responded to the call to prayer, regardless of denomination. It was a massive response by those who had been touched by the wave and had heard the sound!

As these people prayed, angels carrying keys were being released from the places where they were praying. That's when I noticed thousands of people blindfolded and chained to posts all across the nation. The angels with keys unlocked these people from their shackles and removed the blindfolds so they could see. Once freed, the people came and helped us plow.

A war was taking place as we plowed, but it wasn't hard! The plowing was almost effortless, and the hosts of Heaven were easily destroying the demons.

As we continued to plow the ground, we noticed behind us that water and fire were bursting forth. The water shot up like a geyser, and the fire shot up like a volcano erupting. The water did not put out the fire—the water and the fire worked together and were being sprayed out across the entire nation. When the water or fire touched the demons coming up from the tunnel, the demons melted into nothing. The entire scenario was so powerful, and we knew it was contributing to the healing of the land (see 2 Chronicles 7:14 NKJV).

We plowed the ground across the whole United States of America—from the Capitol Building in Washington, DC to the shoreline of the Pacific Ocean on the West Coast.

Everything I have described up to this point happened continuously during the entire journey.

When we reached the coastline of the Pacific Ocean, we stopped plowing, but the roar of the prayer wave kept going, and we knew that people worldwide were being captured by the wave and responding to the call to prayer.

We knew the split in the ground also kept going beyond the shoreline because we could see the waters filling in the void that the split was making as it moved across the ocean floor. For a moment we could see a slight ditch appear in the ocean as the waters were spilling into the split.

Hundreds of thousands of people and angels were now with us, and there was an indescribable rejoicing that filled the atmosphere and entered all the people, and even into the angels.

I noticed a group of people situated somehow in the heavens above us. I recognized Billy Graham, Oral Roberts, and my grandpa. I saw a lady I believed was Maria Woodworth-Etter. Another group of people were the intercessors who prayed with Rees Howells. This group was the great cloud of witnesses, and the indescribable rejoicing even impacted them!

Then we all turned around and looked back toward the East, expecting to see a huge mess. We were not concerned about it, though, because we knew God had done a major work. But when we turned around, everything was perfect. It was as though nothing had even happened. The split in the ground was gone, and the land wasn't even scarred where the split had been. The land was completely whole!

Suddenly, the land—the dirt, trees, shrubs, the grass, the water, all of the land itself—began to sing this well-known chorus: "It is well—with my soul. It is well, it is well with my soul." The land sang this chorus three times. Everyone in the crowd—the people, angels, the great cloud of witnesses, and I–fell to our knees as this holy awe and reverence for God swept over us as the land sang. When the song was finished, we could see God gently swipe His hands together two times, as if dusting off of His hands, and then He spoke in a loud, thundering voice, *"I HAVE DONE IT!"*

End of dream.

What we see happening in our world today cannot be correctly understood by carnal interpretation. It's not carnal; it's spiritual. For years, evil agendas have been working undercover in various ways through various means behind the scenes, in an ultimate attempt to distort, discredit, and remove the truth of the Word of God and to extinguish the light of Christ in this nation and the world.

Principalities and hordes of demonic spirits constantly attempt to dismantle the righteous foundation of this nation. They try to destroy the identity of the nation as it has been determined by God. But their attempts will fail, and hell's agenda will come to nothing! The destiny of God has met with the timing of God, and this preordained meeting is causing an explosion of glory that hell cannot stop!

Be assured that the awakening revival is not a reaction on the part of God against what hell is doing, nor is it an attempt by God in hopes that He may combat hell's operations. No. God is not making things up as He goes along. He is not reacting to what the devil is doing as though satan is calling the shots and God has to spend His time and efforts putting out the devil's fires of rebellion and evil. No! This awakening revival now unfolding was set in place long before satan ever even thought of a plan to try to overthrow God's plan.

God's prophetic declaration in the Garden of Eden rings true and loudly in the ears of satan on a daily basis: *"I will put enmity between you and the woman, and between your seed and her Seed* [Jesus]*; He shall bruise your head, and you shall bruise His heel"* (Genesis 3:15 NKJV). Jesus came, just as God said, and His finished work on the Cross—His death, burial, and resurrection—was for the purpose of destroying the works of the devil (see 1 John 3:8).

Ephesians 1:22 tells us that God has put all things under Jesus' feet. Jesus is the Head of the Body, which is the Church. We are the Body of Christ on earth, and as His Body, He has put all things under our feet, and Paul declares that God is going to use our feet to crush satan (see Romans 16:20). The works of satan that Jesus came to destroy are still destroyed. Victory belongs to Jesus, and Jesus' victory has become our victory.

God is not trying to figure out ways to overcome the devil. Jesus already overcame the devil. God's plan is moving forward, and I am convinced that we have now moved over into a time of acceleration when things will happen very quickly. As Christ's ambassadors, we cannot retreat and try to hide from the evil that has been unleashed on our nation. We must stand up with confidence in our Savior and His assured victory. As the standing Ekklesia, our stand puts pressure on satan's head, ever reminding him of his eternal defeat.

Jesus' victory is our victory.

OPENED EYES AND EARS

Our eyes are open to see truth. Our ears are open to hear the leading of our Guide, and with undaunted confidence in our righteous King Jesus, we boldly put our hand to the plow, and allow God to work through us to dig deep and expose the hidden works of darkness. The battle may be great, but the battle won't be hard. The battle belongs to the Lord! The battle is not a natural battle against flesh and blood; it is a spiritual battle in which the hosts of Heaven are on assignment to assist the saints of God, enabling us to stand as the Church Jesus built, against which the gates of hell cannot prevail. The time of *turning* has come!

Be not afraid and do not be dismayed. Though it may have seemed for a time that satan's plan was prevailing, the truth is his plan is actually unraveling. The Church has found Her voice, and we have returned to our posture of prayer and obedience to God. Shackles are being destroyed. Confining limitations are being removed, and angels are on the move!

The cover-up of satan's agenda is being removed as God's plan of the ages is unfolding, *"The glory of the Lord shall be revealed, and all flesh shall see it together; for the mouth of the Lord has spoken"* (Isaiah 40:5 NKJV). The land is preparing its song of victory, "It is well with my soul," as the healing power of God is administered to restore His order.

Washington, DC, will experience a turning and an awakening to God. Alaska, Hawaii, throughout the Heartland and the northwest states, north to south, east to west, America shall be saved! God has spoken it, and it shall be so! Keep plowing. Keep praying. Keep believing. His plan is in motion, and what God has begun He is faithful to complete!

Let's pray together:

Father, we come boldly into Your presence and acknowledge and decree that You, alone, are God. America is one nation under You, our God. Though the prophetic purposes of our nation seem to be fading into the shadows of an ungodly culture, Your eyes have searched and found within Your Ekklesia hearts that are completely Yours. Through us You will now show Yourself strong with demonstrations of Your love and might to provoke an undeniable awakening to an awareness of You in the Church and in the nation.

We declare that Your original intentions for America are now rising from the shadows to shine once again. You are not late! Your promises for this nation have not been forgotten nor forsaken! Awakening to God has come, and America will revive, be healed, and rise as the nation You birthed her to be. Your determined verdict has been declared and cannot be overruled! Hell's agenda is not hidden from You, and satan will never outwit You. We put our hand to the plow, and You will see to it that every plot, plan, ploy, and scheme of the enemy is uncovered—the hosts of Heaven will be loosed to destroy every work of darkness. What has been sent by hell to destroy Your Church and to stop Your plans for this nation will be ***overturned*** *for Your glory and for our good.*

We stand in faith and agreement with You now to declare that "America shall be saved!" The wells of revival are opened, and the fires of awakening are ignited. The move of God will spread quickly, and all of America will burn with the transforming glory of God, in the name and authority of our victorious King Jesus we pray and declare these things, and it is so!

SECTION FOUR

— 17 —

THE WIND IS BLOWING

No other time in history has demanded the necessity of revealing the true Church as does this moment of time right now. Make no mistake about it, the true Church that Christ made us to be is not a weak entity sitting in hiding, just hoping to hold on until He returns. No. God made us to be a glorious Church, filled and operating with the power of His Spirit. We are people of faith in God. We are filled with fire and clothed in His righteousness, marked and known by the demonstration of His awesome might! As one older minister said, "We were born in the fire, and smoke won't do!"

It's time—time to let the light of His glory come again and expose all the weights, sins, and hindrances that have caused us to be subdued and live below our privilege as Christ's Body. We must cry out for a fresh baptism of the fire of the Holy Spirit, allowing Him to burn off everything that is unlike Him so we are free to run with undeniable signs, wonders, and miracles as He stretches forth His hand through us to draw all people to Himself.

The baton passed to us can and must be carried so that through us God's plan for our times can be fulfilled. We cannot do it on our own, nor can we do it based on what we've always done. We have never passed this way before. It doesn't matter what we think we know about a move of God; we only know in part. Holy Spirit will give us eyes and ability to see beyond what we have known. He empowers and emboldens us to do what we have never done. He is the Wind, and He will fan the embers that will reignite the fire in us and cause it to burn through us to ignite the world with His glory.

Everything is coming together to create a moment like no other. The time is now. The wind is blowing, and we must step into Him and allow Him to carry us, blow through us, and manifest His power.

The next dream and vision I share, give insight to this revelation in greater detail.

— 18 —

RIDE WITH THE WIND

If we live in the Spirit, let us also walk in the Spirit.

Galatians 5:25 KJV

In another dream:

I was walking with a friend in a beautiful area with rolling hills covered with tall, green grass waving in the breeze. I knew there were several other people there with us, though I did not see their faces in the dream. I knew that some of these people were intercessors who have strategically been led by God on many prayer assignments for America.

We walked through the grassy hills and came upon a farm. In the middle of this farm was a huge barn. The walls of the barn were layered with solid gold, and all the trim, including the doors, were painted white.

We approached the barn, and two men stepped out from our group to open the very large doors—one man at each door. They slid open the doors, and we all entered to find that the barn was very clean. There was nothing inside except several horse stalls down both side walls. In each stall was a horse, each with a bridle and saddle. Each horse was prepared to be ridden.

I then heard a man's voice say, "It's time to mount up." His voice was not loud or forceful; he just spoke as a matter of fact.

So we each went to "our" horse. We had been preassigned a horse, and we somehow knew which one was ours. We simultaneously opened our gates to the stalls; as we did, a wind began to blow inside the barn. It grew in intensity, almost becoming a whirlwind. We held tightly to the gates of our stalls to stabilize ourselves. The wind continued to blow inside the barn where it originated, and then began to blow out through the doors.

Eventually we were able to let go of the gates and mount up on our horses. As we did, the man spoke again. This time his voice was a little louder, and there was more of a command in his tone. He said, "It's time to ride with the wind!"

We lined up, and our horses stepped into the wind, and we rode out of the barn.

And that was the end of dream.

BE IN THE WIND

We don't make destiny happen. We move with the timing of God and humble ourselves to walk with God as destiny unfolds, and we learn to recognize and rely on all the things He has made available to us that *"work together for good to those who love God, to those who are called according to His purpose"* (Romans 8:28 NKJV).

In a vision I once had, I saw myself standing in front of a wall with only one window. As I was looking out the window, the Lord spoke to me saying, *"You're standing in front of a window of opportunity right now..."* As I continued looking out, I saw a hand holding an old skeleton key come through the window and put the key in my hand. And then the Lord said, *"...But the window of opportunity is about to become a door of access, and I have given you the key."*

Then all of a sudden the window turned into an arched door. I put the key in the door's keyhole and started to open it. Immediately, a strong wind blew in through the door! I grabbed hold of the door, trying to hold on with everything I had in me. The wind was so strong and boisterous that I was almost knocked off my feet! I cried out, "Jesus, *help* me!"

The Lord said to me, *"This wind is My Spirit, and you must learn how to be in it and how to walk in it."*

The wind was so strong it was taking my breath out of me. I said, "Jesus, I can't even breathe!"

He said, *"You have to learn how to breathe in My Spirit."*

I said, "But, Lord, I can't even move. I can't even let go of this door! How do I learn how to walk in it when I can't even let go or do *anything*?"

Then four angels came—one on each side of me, one behind me, and one in front of me—and the Lord said to me, *"In the days ahead, you have to learn how to BE in My Spirit."*

> I knew He was saying that although I would still be on earth, I would have to learn how to fully recognize and utilize everything He has made available for me to be able to walk in and be in the Spirit.
>
> Those angels were around me, and I found that with their help, I could walk in the wind. I then started taking steps out the door. As I went out the door, blood was dripping on me, and I somehow perceived that it was the day after Passover. I knew that we were going out into something new.

That was the end of this vision.

God is launching the awakened Church into uncharted territory. The window of opportunity is about to become a door of access, and He has given us the key to open that door! I believe the "master key" is faith in God that provokes obedience to God. It is faith to believe that what He has created us to be and do in this moment is not dependent on our might or our power—it's by His Spirit (see Zechariah 4:6). The same Spirit that enabled Jesus to do all He did in His ministry on earth is the same Spirit inside us to enable us to walk out His purposes for our lives in this time. The realm of the Spirit must become more real and familiar to us than the earth realm. We have to learn how to *be* in the Spirit.

The Lord may be saying to you right now, *"Let go of what is holding you back from trusting Me. Learn to be in, walk in, breathe in, and live in the wind of My Spirit!"*

As we go forward, God's prophetic words become weapons that arm us with confidence and peace, knowing that He is with us, that He is empowering us, and that He has equipped us. As Paul instructed Timothy, so Jesus is encouraging us to be inspired and aided by His words—both written and prophetically spoken—so we may fight the good fight (see 1 Timothy 1:18 AMP). When we believe, think on, and speak His words, our way will be made prosperous and we shall have good success (see Joshua 1:8).

God once led me to speak this word of exhortation:

> *Your deliberate interaction with Me in the days ahead will bring you to a dimension and encounter with Me that you have not known. In that place of My presence, you will hear Me. As you hear and adhere to My Word, a door of entrance will be given you into My marvelous Light, and in My Light, you will see light! The Light is My Word. As you see, understanding will be imparted to you! And you will be filled with faith and courage that will launch you in ability and power to live the life I've created you to live and to be the light I've created you to be!*

— 19 —

THE CONCLUSION

Now all has been heard; here is the conclusion of the matter: Fear God and keep His commandments, for this is the duty of all mankind.

Ecclesiastes 12:13 NIV

What do we do with all of these dreams, these words, and these instructions? We pray! We honor God, hear and obey His voice! We stay connected to the right people within the Body so we can give and receive the right supply. We read and believe the written Word of God, the Bible, and build our lives around and upon Its truths. We listen to the true prophets and believe what God says through them. We allow those words—not what the world says—to form our expectations and affect our actions. We stand in a readiness to receive instruction from the Lord and a willingness to follow Holy Spirit's leading.

There is a remnant already postured in this readiness. We are saturated bundles ready to catch and release the fire! Hear the Lord declaring over us today:

Your relentless and persistent pursuit has captured the attention of Heaven. Over you is a portal through which I will now begin to pour out and give entrance to the revealing of My manifested glory. It is the picture of an open Heaven. It is the place of access. Through your prayers, you access Heaven; and through your dedicated lives, Heaven accesses earth! Your pursuit, your sincerity, and your dedication are beginning to unlock the portal even now. As the seal is broken, you are now experiencing just mere droplets of what is to come. What is to come, eyes have not seen, ears have not heard, neither has it even entered into the hearts of men and women what I have prepared. But I say, eyes **will** *see, ears* **will** *hear, and people's hearts will be changed and made glad by what I will reveal in the days and times ahead.*

As the portal opens wider, My glory will come in greater measure than you have ever known or experienced before. What you have read about concerning past moves of My Spirit, you will experience that and even greater. But know this—your prayers and your pursuit of Me will open this portal, and your prayers and your continued pursuit of Me will keep the portal open. What is to come cannot be maintained by the knowledge and ability of people. It is only released, kept, and sustained by the Holy Spirit, My Spirit working in you and through you.

My eyes have run to and fro to find hearts that are turned toward Me. I have found such hearts in you, My intercessors, and now I will begin to show Myself strong on your behalf. This is a divine moment. I say, even now, the seal to the portal is being broken. The flow is beginning. Behold, I come quickly, not to take you away, not yet, but rather to display My glory that all may see and know that I am God!

Awakening revival is beginning. A wave of glory is building. It may be slowly moving at the moment, but it's gaining momentum as the sleeping giant, the Church, is waking up. We are shaking ourselves, and realizing the power deficit that we are experiencing. We see the lack of Christlikeness within the Church. Our spiritual compass must be recalibrated to get us back on track with God's plans and intentions. A remnant is rising with a determination to return to God, so that He may return to us! We are crying out again for the fullness of the glory. We remember the promises. We are provoked by the past moves of God throughout history, and we ask, "Do it again, Lord, in our time!"

We rise with an unrelenting cry that says to God, "Oh, that You would rend the Heavens and come down!" We MUST have Him! We *must* know and be led by Holy Spirit so that His fiery river can continue to flow into us and out through us unhindered. As His governmental Body, Christ has given us keys of authority. As we humble ourselves to walk with Him, to find and know His path and His heart, to hear and heed His instructions, and to encounter Him for ourselves, we can use those keys to bind and to loose what needs to be bound and loosed, and open doors that no one can open and close doors that no one can shut.

It's time. It's time for us to resist compromise. It's time for us to experience and demonstrate Christ and His anointing! It's time for us to shake off complacency, lethargy, and "normalcy," and take courageous leaps of obedience made possible by an unrelenting faith birthed from our total surrender to and focus on God! It's time for us to let go of what has become familiar and comfortable, say "Yes" to Jesus, and ride with the wind of Holy Spirit, allowing Him to guide us in this next Great Awakening!

THE MANTLE OF REVIVAL

I conclude this book by sharing with you one of the most profound dreams concerning revival that I have ever been given. This dream has deeply stirred me. I can't read it or tell it without weeping—not with sadness, but with holy awe and in the fear of the Lord. Oh, His heart is that all people would know Him! How will they know unless they see Him and are told about Him? How will they see His mighty acts and hear of His saving power unless we carry the fire and allow Holy Spirit to reveal the fullness of Christ through us?

The greatest opportunity of our lifetimes is being extended to those who are saved and wholly devoted to Christ and His righteous cause. It is the call to carry the mantle of revival so the fire that came out from God to ignite the Church in the beginning can continue to burn in our time with power and fervency, bringing an undeniable awakening to an awareness of God. We must show up for this moment! We must receive this mantle with honor and the fear of the Lord, and carry it for our generation and for those yet to come. The fire must never go out! We must not allow that to happen!

Though it may seem a daunting, unachievable task, we must allow the move of God to continue. He meant for it *never* to stop! He means for the river to widen, the fire to intensify, and the flow to become even greater! It's here! Awakening has already begun. The alarm is sounding. We've been given the distinct honor of embracing the fiery mantle of awakening revival, and we must *never* allow its purpose to lose its fervency.

When our time is finished, and history records our story, may it be said of us and of our time, "They carried the mantle of revival. Their lives were fuel for the flames of Yahweh, and through them He shined with His power and transforming glory." May the power of God and His mighty acts be experienced and revealed in us and through us, and may the lives we live and the story we leave behind, provoke the generations coming after us to pursue God and to carry the mantle in their time. The cost is great. The mantle is weighty, but the cause is greater—and the revealed glory of God is worth it all.

So I will end with this dream. I will allow the dream to speak for itself. No commentary or interjections...just the revelation of what I believe was actually a holy, prophetic encounter. Put yourself in the dream, put yourself in the story. He's been waiting for you.

In this dream:

> I was with a group of eleven people, including myself. We had been given the opportunity to visit a place that had great significance in revival history. We arrived at an old church built of a grayish/white stone. We stepped inside the church and noticed the wooden floors. I could hear our footsteps as we moved into the sanctuary. We looked around us. The ceilings were high. A balcony surrounded the sanctuary, and a high platform with a very large pulpit was in the center of it. We were walking around slowly, taking everything in and whispering among ourselves about how honored we all were to have been given this amazing opportunity to be in this place, to step on these floors, and to be in this atmosphere that was part of revival history.
>
> We had initially thought we were alone in this sanctuary, but then we heard a man's voice ringing out from behind the pulpit. Although as the people in this dream we could not see the man, as the dreamer of this dream, I could see that he was on his knees with his right hand lifted toward Heaven, and he was in *deep,* travailing prayer. His prayer was so intense and full of passion and sincerity! As he prayed, it seemed he was being emptied out with every word. As he

spoke, he slowly rocked back and forth on his knees, with his hand lifted the whole time. His face was red because of the extreme intensity of his prayer. Probably four or five times, he repeated this same prayer:

"Alas, this cross that I must bear 'tis not a task for me. Its weight is light, for my delight is to do all that You ask of me! I'm turning now...to see Your face; 'tis all that matters to me! I lift mine eyes. LORD, hear my cry: SHOW ME YOUR GLORY!"

As he prayed this prayer over and over, it seemed an electrified current could be tangibly felt, and we were all brought to tears as the weightiness of the presence of God completely filled that room.

I don't have words to really explain this, but the whole atmosphere *filled up* with the pleasure of God. I wish I could articulate better that wonderful experience! We could feel that God was *so pleased* with this man and with this prayer. The feeling of God's pleasure was real and almost tangible. Again, I don't know how to adequately describe that.

Our group reverently walked to our left and sat down on a pew, not wanting to disturb the man who was praying. This is when I looked to my right and noticed that some of those within our group were Pastors Paul and Kim Owens and Larry Sparks.

As the man continued to pray, I was sobbing, overcome by the presence of the Lord. The rest of the group did the same, and the man heard us. He got up off his knees and walked toward the pulpit. I noticed that he was a tall man. He was young, and he was wearing clothing from the early 1900s. The pulpit was very large with a step behind it. The man stepped up onto it and then leaned over the pulpit and saw us there. With his elbows on the pulpit and his face resting in his hands, the man gazed at us and said with deep emotion, almost in a whisper, "You *came*! You're *here*!"

Then he stood up straight, and we saw he was wearing some type of robe, but it wasn't natural clothing. Again, I find it hard to adequately articulate what we saw. The robe was very thick, bulky, and long, touching the floor. I could tell it was old and extremely heavy. He then said to us, "I have been waiting for you!" He put his hand on the robe, and said, "I wore this for my time, and it was all that I desired! *It was* all *that I desired!*"

I was almost afraid to speak, but reverently I asked, "What is it?"

He answered with such respect for it, "It's the mantle of revival!"

"Who are *you*?" I asked.

"That is not important. What *is* important is that you came to get this mantle. You have been sent here for this purpose."

We had thought we were there just to see that building, but we now understood that we had been deliberately, even supernaturally, brought there by God to receive that mantle. That realization was very overwhelming to each of us.

The young man then told us stories about the mantle—the story of how he had received it and stories of the experiences he had while carrying it in his time. We realized this mantle was the "cross" he was so intently speaking about in his prayer. Though heavy, it was not a burden for him; it was the greatest joy of his life!

As he spoke to us, we noticed that the mantle he was wearing was growing. It was extending with every word he spoke. It was filling up the stage. He said, "In my time, I cried out to God and asked for at least 100,000 souls to be touched and changed by the power of God, but in your time it *must be much greater*!" The mantle continued to grow, and he continued to speak. He was giving us instruction and revelation about this mantle because it was being passed to us to carry for *our* time.

As we listened in awe to all he was telling us, the realization hit us that we were going to carry that mantle. We looked at each other astounded, thinking, *We can't carry that! It's too heavy! It's too big!* We were amazed that he was still able to stand under the weight of it as he spoke to us. I was so overcome by the magnitude of what was happening, I was sobbing. I stood up from the pew and stepped out into the aisle and fell on my knees. Everyone in the group did the same.

Knowing that we had for certain been sent by God to receive this mantle, I asked the question that I, along with everyone else, had been thinking. "How can we carry it? It's so BIG!" In the natural, it seemed impossible!

The man answered, "You cannot wear this mantle and look forward or around you. If you do, it will be torn and misused, and it will become cumbersome and even wearisome for you. You must *always* look upward and be *completely* enthralled by the Lord. *Focus* on Him! *Pursue* Him! *Long* for Him, and soon the weight of the mantle will be absorbed by the passion in your heart for more of Him." He then said with profound joy, "Now...it's *your* time to carry the mantle!"

In unison, still weeping, we said, "We receive it! We don't completely know how, but we receive it!" Then out of the depths of our beings, we began to pray that same prayer the man had prayed at the beginning. It rose right up out of us. That prayer became the cry of each of our hearts. We prayed:

"Alas, this cross that I must bear 'tis not a task for me. Its weight is light, for my delight, is to do all that You ask of me! I'm turning now to see Your face; 'tis all that matters to me! I lift mine eyes. Lord, hear my cry: SHOW ME YOUR GLORY!"

The man stepped down from behind the pulpit, back onto the stage, and then he was just gone. (I can't say for certain who the man was, but I have a feeling it may have been Evan Roberts, a young man who was instrumental in the great Welsh revival that took place in the early 1900s. And I feel that Moriah Chapel may have been the church in which we stood.)

Still on our knees, releasing this intense prayer that had now become *our* prayer, that mantle was lifted from the stage and placed on us. It covered us and was now big enough to fill the entire church. As the mantle covered us, it then lifted us up and became like a hang glider of sorts and began to carry us. I could see water beneath us as we were being carried by the mantle over the ocean.

Then we saw land, then mountains, and then we landed, facing westward. With the mantle still covering us, we all knew that we were in the mountains of North Carolina at the place where the Holy Spirit came upon that small group of men in the late 1800s and early 1900s who later launched a couple of the larger Pentecostal denominations. Out in front of us, in the span of about twenty feet in width, we saw white stones making up letters, each about four feet tall, that spelled the words, "TO BE CONTINUED."

That was the end of the dream.

Make this your prayer:

Father, it is not by my might or strength that I don this mantle with which we have been entrusted. I cannot do it on my own, but by Your Spirit, I can run with the fire and flow with Your revival river. I am enthralled by You! I pursue You! I will stay focused on You! I am wholly devoted to You and to Your righteous cause. By the empowerment of Your Holy Spirit, I will carry and release this amazing anointing that will draw people to the knowledge of Christ. I yield to You and to this calling. I humble myself before You and say, "All of me for all of You! Finish what You have started."

With humble obedience, Lord, I receive this sacred mantle, and with deep and intense sincerity I declare:

"Alas, this cross that I must bear 'tis not a task for me. Its weight is light, for my delight, is to do all that You ask of me! I'm turning now to see Your face; 'tis all that matters to me! I lift mine eyes. Lord, hear my cry: SHOW ME YOUR GLORY!"

ABOUT THE AUTHOR

It was at the age of 13 when Gina entered a personal relationship with the Lord Jesus Christ. Hearing testimonies of the "older saints" stirred in her heart a deep desire to know God the way they knew Him. Surrendering her life to the Lord, she was launched into a journey toward fulfilling her God-given purposes. Her spiritual roots run deep in a Pentecostal heritage.

Gina has served in ministry for over 38 years. She is a prophetic minister, who ministers under the anointing and power of the Holy Spirit. Through preaching, prayer, and prophetic declaration, she is contending for an awakening to an awareness of God that will lead to revival and reformation in the Church and in the nation. Gina walks in integrity, seeking only to please the Lord. Her desire is to always honor and bring glory to Jesus Christ alone.

Gina is also a prophetic dreamer. Her dreams and visions have been—and are being—used as strategy for prayer, prayer assignments, and insight to assist the Church in taking Her place to bring an awakening to God in America. Dutch Sheets, Tim Sheets, Chuck Pierce, and others have given voice to many of her dreams and visions in their conferences and ministry platforms by sharing them in their messages, books, social media posts, and podcasts.

Gina is the author of *Awakening the Church to Awaken a Nation*. She is a native of the great state of Tennessee.

TO CONTACT GINA, WRITE TO:

Gina Gholston
P.O. Box 30781
Clarksville, TN 37040

Email: ggministries20@gmail.com

Website: www.ginagholstonministries.org

Facebook: www.facebook.com/ginagholstonministries

YouTube Channel: Gina Gholston Ministries